YOGABLE

A GENTLE APPROACH TO YOGA – FOR SPECIAL POPULATIONS

PATTY (PATWANT) WILDASINN

Illustrations by Israel Ron
Edited by Dr. Dorothy D. Wills
Companion soundtrack by Jap Dharam Rose

BALBOA.PRESS
A DIVISION OF HAY HOUSE

Balboa Press books may be ordered through booksellers or by contacting:

Balboa Press
A Division of Hay House
1663 Liberty Drive
Bloomington, IN 47403
www.balboapress.com
844-682-1282

Because of the dynamic nature of the Internet, any web addresses or links contained in this book may have changed since publication and may no longer be valid. The views expressed in this work are solely those of the author and do not necessarily reflect the views of the publisher, and the publisher hereby disclaims any responsibility for them.

The author of this book does not dispense medical advice or prescribe the use of any technique as a form of treatment for physical, emotional, or medical problems without the advice of a physician, either directly or indirectly. The intent of the author is only to offer information of a general nature to help you in your quest for emotional and spiritual well-being. In the event you use any of the information in this book for yourself, which is your constitutional right, the author and the publisher assume no responsibility for your actions.

The exercises in this book come from the teachings of yoga. No medical advice is intended or given herein. Always check with your personal physician or licensed health care practitioner before making any significant changes in your lifestyle or exercise regimen to ensure that any changes may be appropriate for your personal health condition and for any medication you may be taking.

Any people depicted in stock imagery provided by Getty Images are models, and such images are being used for illustrative purposes only. Certain stock imagery © Getty Images.

ISBN: 978-1-9822-7153-4 (sc)
ISBN: 978-1-9822-7154-1 (e)

Library of Congress Control Number: 2021914069

Print information available on the last page.

Balboa Press rev. date: 08/06/2021

Contents

Acknowledgements

It is with much gratitude that I share *Yogable*. I am grateful for the teachings and technology of Kundalini Yoga, and the teachers, friends, and students I have met along the way. Many thanks to Dr. Gurucharan Singh Khalsa, Dr. Santokh Singh Khalsa, Billy Bang Douglas, Israel Ron, Michael Mejia, Dr. DD Wills, GuruMeher Khalsa and to all of those who contributed by sharing personal testimonials. Special thanks to recording artist and friend, Jap Dharam Rose, for the soundtrack of mantras and music to accompany this book, and for time spent and lessons learned with healer and author Reverend Rosalyn Bruyere.

Much love and thanks to my family for their flexibility and laughter. Most especially to my son who inspired our amazing special needs family yoga classes.

Preface
(Yoga & Able)

"Yogable"
A Gentle Approach to Yoga for Special Populations
Designed for those with special needs, physical limitations, seniors, and families.

Where did this come from?

A spark of motivation came to life as I sat on the beach in Puerto Vallarta, Mexico, where I attended a yoga retreat. Surrounded by stray dogs playing at my feet, I combed through my wet, salty hair and contemplated the question presented by the facilitators, *"What is your gift, what are you going to share?"* A simple answer came to me – *Deliver the message!* The message started with Chapter 8, which I began to write in my notebook on that sun-drenched beach.

The term *"Yogable"* and the title of this book came about from another term I'd been using for well over a decade. I had been fond of telling my students that if you can breathe, you can do yoga, that yoga is "doable" for everyone. One morning while leading a class I accidently said "Yogable" and I knew I'd found a word that could encompass the practices I wanted to share.

As a yoga instructor, I have had the good fortune of making yoga accessible to groups of people with unique abilities (sometimes viewed societally as limitations), senior citizens, those limited to restricted movement, recovering addicts, as well as special needs children and adults, and their families.

The special needs groups include Autism Spectrum Disorder: Autism, pervasive developmental disorder and childhood integrative disorders, in addition to Down Syndrome, ADHD, seizure disorders, Cerebral Palsy, and many others with less commonly known diagnosis. These clients hold a special place in my heart. It is because of my own son's special needs that I found my way to these extraordinary people and those who love them.

Coming out of Kundalini Yoga Level One Yoga Teacher Training, I was in the best shape of my life and ready to teach – *108 frogs! - Let's go! – Keep up!* However, I soon found myself at a local yoga studio teaching "gentle yoga" to a class of seniors with what I perceived as physical "issues." I quickly learned that yoga may be experienced by anyone. I am now the co-owner of this same studio, and I still teach this same class. Today I am able to offer any *kriya* in a gentle way. This is what I want to share - posture, breath, and meditation for all!

This book is a way to share the powerful technology of yoga to populations that may be under-reached and under-served while staying true to the teachings. *Yogable - A Gentle Approach to Yoga for Special Populations* provides an outline for yoga students to experience a supported and doable yoga practice. This book is for both teachers and individual practitioners to peruse and enjoy.

1

An Introduction to Yoga

Yoga is an ancient practice, dating back thousands of years, originally passed from teacher to disciple, maintaining an air of secrecy in the science. The first assembled record of yoga dates back approximately 2,000 years when yogi and sage, Maharishi Patanjali, outlined the yoga *sutras* in written form. The *sutras* are like packets of information detailing the lifestyle, practices, and benefits of yoga. The history of yoga is much broader than one person. Its threads can be seen in the Hindu tradition within the Upanishads, early yoga writings that weave back through Vedic science which is an ancient Indian philosophy. The *sutras* are the first comprehensive written compilation of the complete yoga experience, detailing the prescribed practice for connecting to inner wisdom. Over the past 500 years, yoga has slowly made its way out of isolation and into the service of humankind. During the last century yoga has evolved, coming into this age, spreading to benefit people worldwide.

I took my very first yoga class in San Francisco in the mid 1970's. Okay, so I was 9 years old, visiting my great aunt for spring break. Evidently, yoga was not to be missed, even with a visiting child in the house. One evening during my stay, I was taken out to a basement yoga class, packed with old ladies in leotards standing on their heads. I was cautiously observant in this dim, crowded basement. Mind you, I am now probably older than most in that room full of "old ladies," but when you're 9 all adults seem old. I remember being quite impressed that my great aunt could perform a head stand, and even more impressed that her roommate was the yoga teacher. I did not return to a yoga class until shortly after I was 30, but the 1970's San Francisco experience just makes for a cool, hip story.

When I did stumble back into yoga, these two sweet women who were by then in their 80's, my great aunt Betty and her yoga teacher roommate, were so happy and supportive of my endeavor to practice and teach.

Looking back some 20 years, I do feel I was divinely guided into a yoga class. I don't recall making any conscious decision to be there or begin the practice. I did, however, make an immediate conscious decision to jump into the journey with both feet. I began with Kundalini Yoga and quickly expanded my practice to include Hatha Yoga and Yoga Nidra, as well as the early 2000's fad of Power Yoga. I loved the eclectic mix, and some days I sure miss the power yoga body I had back then. Ultimately, I was drawn to train formally in Kundalini Yoga. The *kriyas* and meditations resonate in my being. This book reflects my early practice, in that I draw from the whole, large pool of yoga, especially in creating a fun and expansive practice for special needs kids and families. It is however, delivered with the experience and wisdom of my practice today, and all I have learned along the way.

Kundalini yoga is known as the yoga of awareness. It is a precise technology and science of the body, mind and spirit. All forms of yoga tap into the reserve of Kundalini energy held within the body, with the intent being energy integration. It works to clear, heal, and integrate the practitioner. Although the practice is precise, it is also very forgiving. If you can breathe, you can practice yoga. Yoga itself comes from the word *yoke* which in the Hindu tradition implies union through physical and spiritual practice. By doing yoga, one helps to unite body, mind and spirit. From there, union can be extended to include the Divine. Time to throw in a disclaimer: yoga is a spiritual, not religious practice. It may help to think of it this way - religion takes place in a building, while spirituality is something God-given by virtue of being human. A yoga practice should support and enhance whatever your current beliefs and faith may be, and all denominations are welcome. There is no particular belief or faith required to practice. If perhaps you are feeling that a symbiotic relationship between you and the world around you is not currently accessible, you just may find something you've been looking for in yoga.

Kundalini energy itself is a spiritual energy that flows through our bodies at all times; it's merely the frequency and intensity that vary from individual to individual. Kundalini energy is like the crystal in the timepiece that keeps the clock running. There is a reserve of Kundalini energy that resides near the base of the spine, and is represented as a coil. It is both grounding and uplifting at the same time. Yoga distributes this life force energy throughout the entire body.

This all sounds great, you may say, but where is the practicality?

Yoga is actually a highly practical approach to the body and the mind, and, as taught today, is for those of us who live within the realm of human society; we have families, friends, jobs, social engagements, and responsibilities to others. Most people today do not have the time (or the desire) to go off and live in a cave and meditate for twenty years, waiting to achieve enlightenment. The yoga *kriyas,* or sets, and meditations outlined in this book are a very direct application, tapping into the nervous system, stimulating the body on a glandular and cellular level. Have you ever felt like you are being run over by life, that time is moving too fast, or that you simply are not in control? The practice of yoga strengthens the nervous system so that the body and mind may more easily synchronize with the flow of life, with flexibility and resiliency, relieving feelings of being overwhelmed or being bulldozed. It works on the entire being through *pranayam* (breath), *asana* (posture), and meditation, which may include *mantra* (chanting) and *mudra* (hand positions), and relaxation.

These yogic techniques are combined with an emphasis on coordinating breath and posture to create an experience. It's not about twisting yourself into a pretzel to attain a difficult posture in order to admire how great you look while practicing. The focus of yoga is the experience - the benefits you receive in class and what carries over into your daily life. The coordination of breath and posture, meditation and relaxation, is what accounts for glandular stimulation and cleansing, which induces a feeling of renewal or being refreshed after yoga practice. Simultaneously, muscle and tissue work to create strength and flexibility, while meditation works to cleanse the subconscious and direct the wavelengths of the brain.

At the same time, the work goes deeper than the body and mind, to a place within the soul. In the practice of yoga, it is believed that the *soul body* is our own inner guiding light, the part of us that longs for union with the Divine. In Ayurveda (ancient Indian medicine,) the soul is thought to be a tiny spark of light found in the heart center. I think of the soul as the pulse of life - the pulse that beats deep within, that drives us to create, that spreads ripples connecting us all to each other and to life itself.

Why is the soul important to a gentle approach to yoga? Well, because yoga is all-encompassing. It is the union of body, mind, spirit, as well as union with the Divine, union with the pulse of life. We are an expression of the Divine.

When we see humanity, our communities, our friends, and our families as part of one huge pulse of life, we come to understand a basic truth: that we all want to feel loved and connected, part of something greater than ourselves. And, if we all want the same things and if yoga encompasses all, then there are no absolutes. Yoga is accessible to all in this day and age. Work where you are and make daily decisions on your current practice. Modifications and choices provide a roadmap for inclusion and empowerment! This "all" is the essence of *Sat Nam*.

Sat Nam is a frequently used mantra. We link it with the breath for focus and chant it at the close of each class. *Sat Nam* means *truth is my identity*. This truth is bigger than you and me; it is Universal. *Sat Nam* is a seed (or *bij)* mantra, powerful in its simplicity and all inclusive.

In conversation with my yoga teacher and mentor, Gurucharan Singh Khalsa, Ph.D., he speaks of making yoga accessible to all by *"adapting while remembering the thread,"* stating *"there's precision and there's application, modify with consciousness."*

A yoga practice is not about perfecting posture, looking good, or performing the "right" meditation. The practice is about the experience of connecting to and using body, mind and spirit together. It's about being and embracing who you are and not comparing your *insides* to other people's *outsides*. This book is a guide to a practical approach to practice for all levels and abilities.

Though one is likely to feel some immediate results from the yoga, please remember that the practice is a process: ever growing and deepening with each practitioner over time. Connect with the present moment and start where you are!

2

A Window into the Aura

Including observations as shared by Reverend Rosalyn Bruyere

"I AM a being of energy that knows myself through the consciousness of my chakras."
- Geoffrey Jowett (2014)

On this amazing yogic, and parenting, journey I have had the privilege to connect with healer Reverend Rosalyn Bruyere. She has worked on my son energetically throughout his life. She has been generous with her time on both a professional and personal level. In observing my family yoga classes she has shared a wealth of information regarding the energetic impact of yoga on individuals with special needs and beyond. With her permission, I am immensely grateful to be able to share her observations.

Rosalyn L. Bruyere, founder of the Healing Light Center Church in Southern California, is an ordained minister, internationally known healer, clairvoyant, and medicine woman. She was an instrumental pioneer, consultant, and part of the original experiment on the aura with Dr. Valerie Hunt at UCLA in the 1970's. UCLA facilitated the first of its kind, eight-year research conducted on the human electromagnetic field. Rosalyn is the author of *Wheels of Light, Chakras, Auras, and the Healing Energy of the Body* (1994).

In addition to sharing observations from Rosalyn, I also share insight based on my own personal experience and interactions from teaching thousands of Kundalini classes. I do not attempt to give a complete or comprehensive presentation on developmental delays, nor do I present scientific data with regard to the flow of energy. Rather, the information is shared from a yogic perspective, from my own participation, and from personal lessons learned. What Rosalyn visualized validates the energetic shifts I sense and feel from yoga, along with the benefits extolled throughout the history of yoga.

Definitions of chakras and the aura:

"Chakra is a Sanskrit word used by the Hindus. It literally means 'wheel of light.' Each chakra has four discernible characteristics that functionally affect the aura: color, size and shape, rotation or spin, and intensity (or amount of energy produced.) As a chakra spins, it produces its own electromagnetic field, which combines with the fields generated by the other chakras to produce what we call the auric field."

– compiled from Wheels of Light by Rosalyn L. Bruyere (1989)

"Chakra means 'wheel.' Chakras are energy centers, or energy vortices. They exist as dynamic energies, and they can help us to understand the way energy is processed by a human being within the vast and complex interplay of a multi-leveled existence. The eighth chakra is the aura. It appears to be an oval or a circle of light. The aura combines the effects of all the other chakras."

– from The Aquarian Teacher (Yogi Bhajan 2003)

To put my own spin on it, (pun intended), chakras are spinning fountains of energy that influence the body on a physical, emotional, mental and spiritual level. They are deeply tied to our health and well-being. Yoga typically refers to the seven main chakras which vibrate along the spinal column, and the aura as chakra number eight, as I will also, for the purpose of this chapter. The chakras have a home base that corresponds to locations along the spinal column, but they do not function exclusively independent. The chakras interact with one another to optimize overall balance throughout and beyond the body. Each person vibrates their own unique auric personality. The color and strength of the aura is a projection of the chakras, energy centers of the body, and this color and intensity is in turn a direct projection of what is going on physically, emotionally, and spiritually within each person at any given moment. Yoga acts directly on the chakras, stimulating energy flow and integration. The aura is not static, but ever-changing.

A healthy aura can extend 9 feet around the body in all directions. The primary, or inner, aura extends out around the body approximately 4-5 inches. This primary aura can be felt and experienced by anyone. Let's try a little experiment now. Begin by rubbing the palms together briskly until heat is created, then bring the palms facing each other, about 6 inches apart, in front of the body. From here, begin to slowly move the palms toward each other and back out, palpating the air between for a gentle resistance. When you come up against a slight resistance, as if you're holding a bubble, this is where the edges of the primary aura meet. This will give you an idea of the size of your inner aura. From here the aura extends out in all directions. Although an edge to the aura can be sensed, it does continue to subtly penetrate and interweave through the universe. The penetration and expression of the aura originate from within the body.

The projection of the aura in regard to color and size radiates from the energy centers within; however, it is important to keep in mind that everything we come in contact with affects our energy field. For instance, fresh air, pure water, and positive, supportive people contribute to clarity and health. Conversely, waves from the constant stream of technology (cell phones, computers, microwave, etc.), pollution, and negativity may weaken the aura and be taxing on overall health. On all levels, what we consume we create, including the energy centers within the body.

Let's move back within to the chakras and take a look at the basic location, color, element, and quality of each energy center. In addition, we'll identify clues that may help to determine if each chakra is in or out of balance, and yoga postures to support each center. The information that follows is fundamental, just the tip of the iceberg, but can be helpful in visualization and basic understanding of the chakra system.

CHAKRA BASICS

First Chakra: Muladhara – The Root of Foundation

Location: Base of the Spine
Color: Red. Bone marrow chi (energy) is red and regenerates during sleep.
Element: Earth
Sense: Smell
Qualities: Basic desire for safety, Fight or flight response, Habitual patterns, Foundation for life
Physical: Elimination, Adrenals, Bones, Feet, Rectum, Large intestine
Unbalanced: Fear, Unstable constitution, Addictive behavior, Tunnel vision, Self-centered, Feelings of not belonging, Insecurity
Balanced: Secure, Loyal, Trust, Living in the moment, Valuing oneself, Self-awareness, Stability, Confidence, Feeling of being grounded
Yoga Postures: Crow, Chair, Frogs, Front stretches

Second Chakra: Svadhistana – Sweetness

Location: Sacral spine, about 2" below the navel
Color: Orange. Bone vibrates orange. Exercise clears and builds bone and moves emotion through the body.
Element: Water
Sense: Touch
Qualities: Creativity, Empowerment, Sexuality, Desire, Relates to change and flow of life, Motion, Passion for life and hobbies
Physical: Bodies are formed and carried here, Kidney, Bladder, Reproductive organs
Unbalanced: Shallow relationships, Shame, Sexual irresponsibility, Guilt, Rigidity
Balanced: Responsible relationships, Creative, Ability to express intimacy, empathy & passion, Sense of others, Patience, Joy, Contentment
Yoga Postures: Frogs, Cobra, Butterfly, Cat-cow

Third Chakra: Manipura – Lustrous Gem, Will of Spiritual Warrior

Location: Solar plexus, about 2" above the navel
Color: Yellow. Yellow is a mental color, and can be used to support learning.
Element: Fire
Sense: Sight, both physical and creative.
Qualities: First link to life, Physical health, Personal power, Will, Logic, Reason, Assimilation, Judgement, Integration

Physical: Digestive organs, Muscles
Unbalanced: Greed, Anger, Despair, What's in it for me attitude
Balanced: Inner balance, Self-esteem, A sense of command over life, Leadership skills, Stability, What's in it for us attitude
Yoga Postures: Stretch pose, Bow, Fish, Breath of Fire

Fourth Chakra: Anahata – Unstruck

Location: Heart Center
Color: Green. The skeletal muscles vibrate green.
Element: Air
Sense: Touch
Qualities: Expansiveness, The middle way, Compassion, Unconditional love, Kindness, Truth, Clarity, Balance, Transition
Physical: Heart, Thymus, Arms, Hands, Lungs
Unbalanced: Grief, Loneliness, Hurt, Attachment, Dependent, Guarded emotionally
Balanced: Love, Harmony, Acceptance, Detachment, Forgiveness, Neutrality, Self-love, Service
Yoga Postures: Heart opening postures, Baby pose, Arm work

Fifth Chakra: Vishudda – Purification

Location: Throat
Color: Blue. The fascia vibrates blue.
Element: Ether
Sense: Sound
Qualities: Personal domain, Creative destiny, Communication, Truth, Expression, Language, Subtle connection
Physical: Throat, Neck, Shoulders, Thyroid, Parathyroid
Unbalanced: Manipulative, Shy, Overly bold in speech, Expression problems, Insecurity, Frustration
Balanced: Healthy expression, Authentic, Truthful, Effective, Ability to hear what's not said
Yoga Postures: Neck work, Mantra.
Additional: Honey is also good for this chakra.

Sixth Chakra: Ajna – Perception

Location: Between, in the center, and slightly above the line of the eyebrows
Color: Indigo, Deep purple, Dark plum
Element: Beyond gross elements

Sense: Intuition
Qualities: Soul attached here, Where the inner teacher sits, Beyond duality, Oneness, Spirit,
Physical: Autonomic nervous system, Higher glands, Eyes, Brain
Unbalanced: Confusion, Unclear, Depression, Feeling "out of it," Lack of focus
Balanced: Clear perception and vision, Reliable intuition, Focused, Complete, Comfort with self
Yoga Postures: Forehead to the floor, Meditation

Seventh Chakra: Sahasrara – Infinite

Location: Crown of the head
Color: White or bright violet
Sense: Divine
Qualities: Container for life force, Oneness, Humility, Knowing, Vastness, Divine wisdom
Unbalanced: Doubt, Confusion, Denial of the spiritual realm, Religious extremism, Alienation,
Fear of death
Balanced: Unity, Elevation, Bliss, Surrender, Connection, Conscious of the Infinite, Ability to
let go
Yoga Postures: Focus at the tip of the nose, Meditation

Eighth Chakra: Radiance

Location: Electromagnetic field, Aura, Weaves through the universe
Color: Projection from the chakras
Sense: Being
Qualities: Protects and projects, Positive attraction, Repels negativity, Buffer
Balanced: Filters out negative influences, Protection
Unbalanced: Withdrawn, Feeling vulnerable
Yoga Postures: Down-dog (Triangle), Arm work, Meditation
Additional: To maintain vitality and range of color frequencies you need to stretch yourself
by doing something new. Individual frequency needs to be higher than everything that moves
through it. If you're not actively engaged in learning or growing you lose aura and life force.

What is the aura-yoga connection?

In an attempt to remain succinct and clear, I will attempt to keep it simple. Yoga works on the
aura or magnetic field. The aura extends out around the entire body and provides each person
with a buffer between themselves and the world around them. The aura is a vibration designed
for protection, and it acts as a filter. A strong aura is flexible in nature. It filters out and repels

negativity while attracting and integrating positivity. Very simply, yoga affects the aura in a positive way and strengthens its function.

If the aura is weak or not functioning properly, an individual may not receive adequate protection and be left open to unwanted energies. In yoga, we work to strengthen the aura, ideally working to create an intact, smooth magnetic field that surrounds the entire body. Special needs individuals have more weaknesses and peculiarities in their auras than the general population. Yoga helps to fortify the protective field and improve sensory processing.

Even though my focus is on helping the special needs population, the information in this chapter applies to everyone. As humankind continues to evolve, greater intuition is needed to integrate the surrounding environment, which can be developed through meditation. It is my observation that even today's neuro- typical youth are vibrating with a greater sensitivity than generations past. The Earth's transition into the Age of Aquarius contributes to this increased sensitivity, but that's another book for another author. Let's just say the days of *"Suck it up"* are over with today's children and youth. Believe me, I've tried it to no avail. And, those with processing issues will push back with increased resistance.

Inspirational speaker and author, Esther Hicks, credited as Abraham Hicks, addresses the increase of individuals being born in this day and age who are vibrating with a greater sensitivity than in generations past (2008). These individuals are showing up as teachers, here to help us usher in a time of awakening. In a way, they are forcing this awakening by their complete resistance to fit into society's mold of what is deemed civilized and socially acceptable. Many clips of Abraham's talks on autism and special needs can be found online on YouTube. The main idea presented is that those with special needs are showing up unapologetically as who they really are; allowing, holding a vibration to their true self, unwilling to be forced into being someone they are not, and living free. She states what society calls "normalcy" is conditioned conformity. The lesson delivered from these highly sensitive people is deep, unconditional love and freedom.

Individuals with ASD and other sensory processing disorders fall within a huge spectrum of abilities, strengths and weaknesses. There is no one size fits all. Some persons on the spectrum are able to be successful in the workplace and self-supporting as adults, and others are non-verbal and require 24 hour a day care for their very basic needs that will last a life time. Those on the spectrum may not be able to discern social cues and avoid social contact, or may be overly touchy feely. Eye contact may be completely absent or averted, or conversely may be a too direct, blunt stare. To reiterate from the past paragraph, they typically don't care about being classified as outside of the norm because they are living authentically. We can help to support functioning in society while respecting the individual.

For example, for those who have difficulty with direct eye contact, it is important not to force the issue. Forced eye contact has been described by one young man with ASD as an invasion of the soul. We want to invite people into the practice, not push them away, so keep in mind the spectrum is broad and varied. Throughout this book I will invite you to challenge but not force. One major commonality, regardless of the level of functioning, is the expression of the aura.

Autism Spectrum Disorder (ASD) may encompass symptoms of extreme sensitivity and sensory overload. As mentioned, individuals may resist compliance within society, parents, teachers, etc. They may protect themselves by contracting their aura, or pulling it in tight, in order to block out energy and triggers around them. This is done instinctually and on a subconscious level. According to Rosalyn Bruyere, typically people who are Autistic (and those with sensory processing issues) have a concentrated aura projecting up and out from the forehead, the third eye area, in the shape of a purple tube. With the aura concentrated here, it does not extend down to provide smooth, all-over body coverage. Without the aura properly surrounding the body, individuals may feel perpetually exposed and super-sensitive. Their vulnerable bodies may protect themselves through unusual behaviors: aggression, what may look like tuning out completely, or stimming, which is any repetitive, self-soothing action such as flapping arms or hands, or rocking the body. This resistant response or behavior is not by choice, but is a function of survival in a big, sensory-filled world. A contracted aura keeps others out, and stimming behavior is an attempt to regulate personal energy.

Yoga and meditation can be self-soothing too, as they require no outside touch. Yoga and meditation help to boost, smooth, and spread the aura around the body. There is a meditative practice outlined in chapter 8 that serves as a wonderful example of a self-healing technique that literally moves the aura from its concentration at the forehead, up and over the head and down along the back. The movement is very similar to one used by healers to build auric coverage along the spinal column for those with weaknesses in the aura. Due to sensitivity at the third eye, it may be uncomfortable for those with ASD, and others with sensory processing issues, to have others put their hands in or around the space in front of the forehead. Therefore, the self-regulated movement in yoga and meditation, where each individual chooses how much or how little they engage in the postures, allows students to participate to tolerance. The parent or teacher is not trespassing into the student's auric field, but giving them techniques for self-healing and strengthening the aura. Honestly, the students just think they are having fun; they don't need lengthy explanations of the healing qualities of yoga.

An interesting fact: In American Sign Language, the sign for "Autism" is a gesture indicating "going within" or "remaining within."

In addition to what modern day science tells us yoga does for the body, I wanted to know what changes yoga posture and meditation create in the aura. If yoga physically stretches and strengthens muscles and tissues, stimulates the glands, balances the nervous system, and invokes an overall sense of well-being, what then, is happening in color to the energetic field? I asked Reverend Bruyere to observe my special needs yoga class for the purpose of feedback and education.

She first observed that everyone came into class with their own auric colors, each different. Typically, those with Autism and sensory issues projected a purple tube of energy up and out from the forehead. As soon as we tune in with *Ong Namo Guru Dev Namo,* everyone's aura turned blue, special needs or not.

I was personally delighted to hear this because blue is a fifth chakra color. The activation of this color in the throat center, and subsequently the aura, supports communication, creativity, authentic expression, connecting, hearing, and listening. We all started class on the same page, at the same time, once we communicated via *Ong Namo Guru Dev Namo.* Our sacred *Adi Mantra* is a great equalizer!

When a class, as a group, moves into posture, the aura and color changes are universal for all participants. Some individuals have a stronger response than others, but the areas activated by yoga posture created similar color changes in each student. What is significant to note is that in the special needs population, the primary aura expands to a normal four-to-five inch range while in the yoga posture, and then contracts when resting between postures. This auric contraction is thought to be a form of self-defense. When the student auras are full-sized, it's easier for outside influences, such as parents, teachers, peers, society, and environment, to get in and create the feeling of "being pulled at," which triggers discomfort. Yoga posture does ignite the aura, and a yoga class can be a safe place to experience these changes and build tolerance to the expanded, or more normal sized aura.

I want to acknowledge and comment on the contradictions here in aura protection. I have said that ideally the aura extends around the entire body providing protection, and I have also said that some special needs persons energetically contract the aura for protection in terms of comfort. Comfort does not equal adequate energetic processing and balanced healthy auric protection. We all need to stretch ourselves and move out of our comfort zones to grow and to keep our life force strong.

Examples of yoga posture and meditation that affect color changes in the aura:

The yoga practices in the examples given below are outlined throughout this manual, and are given in detail in the pages to follow. The colors described are as seen as expressed in the aura.

1. Tuning-in with the opening mantra (*Adi Mantra*) and postures that induce a relaxed upper body while seated create the color blue. As mentioned, when students chant *Ong Namo Guru Dev Namo* to prepare for class, all the auras present turn blue. This includes the non-verbal participants.
2. Working and moving the arms activates green, a heart center color. This color moves from the center of the chest down through the arms. The arms and hands are an extension of the heart center.

3. Pelvic Rotation activates orange in the second chakra, the lower abdomen, which radiates around the lower torso. This brings students into their bodies where life is experienced. Ideally, this is where we should all be in relation to our bodies, connected to and radiating from the core. Continued practice of Pelvic Rotation activates the color orange down into the legs, too.

4. Poses that activate the color red include work with the feet, legs and balance, such as Tree Pose, coming up and down on the toes, and squats or jumping. Red energy comes up from the ground into the legs. This is helpful for grounding. Poses that work with the feet, lifting or positioning, also activate the brain. Archer pose, for instance, fires the brain and brings students into the present moment.

5. Dancing and swaying while standing ignites the color lavender in the aura, a projection from third eye and crown. When we listen to the body and dance, our bodies intuitively know how to move in order to bring balance both physically and energetically.

6. The *Kirtan Kriya* Meditation mentioned throughout this book was observed in class, and by the end of the meditation the group was vibrating purple. Kids are very good at mantra, even those who don't have command of standard spoken language. Mantra is a powerful tool, and kids do well with music, chanting and singing along with the sound current. Expose children to different mantras and songs and let them choose what they like. They will intuitively know what mantra best fits their needs.

At the end of a traditional and vigorous adult Kundalini yoga class, the majority of students will have activated red, or pink, in the aura radiating from the first and seventh chakras. Remember all of the chakras are stimulated with each yoga kriya, but the red color indicates that the Kundalini energy is being projected. This is a phenomenon I have, on occasion, personally observed.

With kids, it is interesting to note during class when one gets to where they're going in terms of posture and energy, the group quickly shifts and follows along. They move as a group, their energy supporting one another. The flow is cohesive. This happens naturally, with no thought or knowledge, in children and those of all ages with special considerations. The accompanying adults don't access this subconscious cohesive flow as easily as their children.

The parents or those caring for children/adults with special needs on a regular basis don't shift as easily with the group due to a subtle containment of energy. Energetic resistance is not demonstrated on an emotional level, nor is it intentional, but the aura is most closely related to the emotion of fear. Fear creates an invisible shield of protection, a set of armor that is difficult to penetrate when it is not expressed on a conscious level. Parents who expend all of the strength necessary to raise a special needs child are often reluctant, on a subconscious level, to care for themselves. A safe place to let go and renew can be a special gift bestowed by the practice of yoga.

Let's take a deeper look at the aura relationship between the mother and child. Yogic philosophy teaches that when a child is born, the aura of the mother and child are not separate. Ideally, the auras remain connected for the first few years of life. Around the age of three, the child begins to enter a contrary phase, questioning *"why"* at every opportunity, thus beginning the aura separation process. Even though my son is now in his twenties, I've often commented that I feel like I have a perpetual three-year old! The auric separation that begins around age three is not complete, as the mother and the child will always be linked on a subtle level through emotion. This auric connection presented herein is given as a predictable energetic process of typical growth. It is important to note that even typical patterns can differ immensely for every relationship.

The separation of auras may be delayed, if not curtailed completely, when developmental delays are present in the child. Mothers tend to keep special children in close to their aura. This is in an attempt to try to control behavior and protect the child. It can be helpful to simply be aware that the energetic sensitivity and enmeshment may be increased between mother and the special needs child. The demands on the mother's aura can be downright draining, and what the mother experiences is transferred to the child on an energetic level. Clearly, this reason alone explains why it is so important for the mother to find balance for herself. The child picks up on the energy and emotion rather than the words and actions of others around them; mom, dad, siblings, grandparents, teachers, etc. This is true for all young children, but can be lifelong for the child/adult with developmental delays or special gifts. It's like being entangled together, where thoughts, vibrations, and emotions directly affect one another.

This vibrational interaction is actually always happening, with everyone. With maturity and growth, the neuro-typical individual is easily able to filter this static out in day-to-day activities, tuning in only when necessary. The relationship between special needs kids and their parents remains, for the most part, at full volume and intensity, which quite frankly is exhausting.

To reiterate, the so called "norm" can be viewed as a wide and diverse spectrum in itself. Cases of disassociation, where the parent is not available to the child on an energetic or nurturing level do exist, and do not fall into the "norm" of the flow of energy outlined within this chapter. "Normal" is scientifically calculated with a fairly low percentage of people actually falling right in the middle of the measurement that calculates what we call average or typical. We're all unique, as are the needs of children.

When children are in crisis at any age or developmental ability, the close mother/child auric connection may be activated and projected as a means of protection. Parents of typical adult children may experience a lingering auric connection and separation later in life due to any number of circumstances. Some kids and adults weave in and out of the protection of the mother's aura as needed. Most of this takes place outside the realm of concrete awareness.

The mother/child aura connection may be established with children who are adopted, just as with biological parents. In yoga it is believed that all children end up with their parents, the persons their soul agreed to, regardless of biology. The mother energy is about nurturing, creating, and love, which can include sacrifice. Mother, or divine feminine energy, resides in all women and is not activated only by childbirth. It is accessible to all women.

Due to this auric connection between mother and child, a mother who meditates reaps the benefit for her children as well as herself. Through this beautiful link the mother can hold space in meditation to continue to support and encourage the child, even into adulthood for all levels of development. There may be situations in which parents feel powerless or helpless in the physical realm, but the higher realm of meditation is always accessible. It is not the job of the mother or the yoga teacher to fix anything. We are who we are, this is our personal journey, there is no judgement placed. Meditation may help in navigating the journey.

Special needs children are especially sensitive to a mother's meditation practice and this may be observed in their behavior. This healing work is not always easy; sometimes it's actually emotionally messy, but as I have experienced, it is well worth the effort. One of the challenges for parents may be to find the time to meditate in an already busy life. This is where a family style yoga class comes in handy, providing a safe place for the whole family to practice a little self-care together.

Meditating fathers make an impact too! Although fathers do not have the same auric connection with their children, their participation in family yoga delivers a strong message of approval and acceptance, and is sweet to observe. Kids light up when dad comes along to yoga!

The goal of imparting this information is the development of individual awareness and self-empowerment. To identify the need for self-care without guilt! To claim personal power! The need for compassionate self-care holds true for both the parent and the yoga teacher facilitating the yoga experience. With understanding and compassion for self and others, we can give ourselves space to simply be, to relax and recharge for another day. Ignorance may sometimes be seen as bliss, but it is also related to darkness or lack of knowledge. A little bit of knowledge and awareness can lead to light and expansion. Once self-knowledge is awakened, the power of choice is available as we listen to our true needs.

Meditation works on the heart center where the neutral mind, or truth, resides. Whereas the continued practice of yoga strengthens the body on a physical and energetic level, a continued practice of meditation brings the heart center into balance, so inner truths may be heard. Through consistent practice, tolerance is built and longer times of meditation and relaxation may be achieved. I suspect this is along the lines of *what you fire you wire* in relation to the chemistry of the brain. The practice of yoga gives students tools to build the aura for strength, protection, and harmony. And, who couldn't use a little harmony in life? A strong aura also helps us in keeping up with life's demands and celebrations.

3

Tuning In; Ong Namo, Guru Dev Namo

"Remember ...the entrance to the sanctuary is inside you."

- Rumi (2003)

At the beginning of each class or personal practice, I recommend what is called "tuning-in" by chanting the words of the *Adi Mantra - Ong Namo, Guru Dev Namo*. In doing so, we are preparing for our experience, bowing to the Highest Consciousness as we call upon our own Divine Wisdom or inner-teacher. The *Adi Mantra* connects us to the Divine Flow of Life, as well as the teachings and the teachers of past, present and future. Ultimately, we pause with reverence and chant to connect with the Divine Flow of Life – the Pulse of Life.

It is worth noting that we are actually never disconnected from the Divine Flow of Life, we sometimes just get busy and forget that we are connected.

This opening mantra is user friendly. When calling upon the Highest Consciousness, it is whatever each person believes and experiences. We do not bow to what someone else believes or what the teacher believes. We simply offer the mantra as we bow to a Universal Wisdom without intending to define it for others.

Traditionally, tuning in is done while seated in Easy Pose with the hands in Prayer Pose. In Prayer Pose, the palms of the hands come together at the center of the chest, or heart center. The palms connect with light pressure and the thumbs rest on the sternum. The purpose of this posture is not actual prayer, but rather the calming effects the *mudra* (hand position) has on the body and mind. Prayer Pose helps to increase communication between the hemispheres of the brain, and supports balance and neutrality. Resting in a neutral space for a few moments at the beginning of class is a good time to set an intention, if desired.

Alternately, tuning in may be done with the hands resting down on the knees in any seated posture. Setting intention is not required. Teachers trained in a Hatha tradition may prefer to use the mantra *Om*.

What is the difference between *Om* and *Ong*? *Om* refers to the entirety of Creation and is passive. *Ong* refers to the Creator and is assertive. It's like comparing the infinite to the finite. *Om* may foster feelings of peace and calm, whereas *Ong* offers activation and the power to get the job done. Both mantras vibrate connection to the Divine, but since our human nature is finite we chant *Ong* in the Kundalini tradition.

When teaching children, I describe tuning in as bowing to the Highest Good or Ultimate Good. They may not understand vocabulary such as "consciousness," and it doesn't matter because kids understand what's good. Keep it simple! There will be more later on translating *mantras*, especially *Sat Nam,* so the kids don't start calling you "Miss Truth." True story!

The ability to speak is not a prerequisite for tuning in. Non-verbal students can tune in, and it is quite powerful! Every week I have the privilege of listening to and feeling non-verbal kids, teens, and adults tune in to class with the vibration of sound without actual words.

When working with children and adults with special needs, I'm looking to activate energy to get the job done, so I use the *Adi Mantra* when beginning class. The special needs community does not hold back; everyone belts out their best *Ong Namo, Guru Dev Namo.* It is simultaneously the worst and most beautiful thing you'll ever hear. It may assault the ears, but make the heart and soul expand with love and joy.

The power of this mantra is included in the book because of the positive effect it has on the aura, and its ability to center and ground students prior to practice. There need not be any specific belief or tradition affiliated with the mantra. The mantra is made up of words with a powerful vibration, but words nonetheless. Humankind speaks different languages all over the world; this is a derivative of the Sanskrit language found to have a high vibration.

That being said, there may be teaching settings that do not allow for the use of mantra, such as schools, church groups, or scouting organizations. Kundalini yoga teachers may feel somewhat resistant to foregoing a traditional tune-in, but teachers of other traditions and those engaging in personal practice may have no issues skipping a mantra to begin class. There are options for teaching in settings that don't allow the use of mantra, and each individual teacher will need to decide and reconcile with what is comfortable for them.

A great way to introduce *Ong Namo, Guru Dev Namo* is to play the mantra in the room as you are preparing to teach and as the students are setting up for yoga. This sets the tone for class and opens the door for singing along to the mantra with music. The same principle can apply for a personal practice, following along with the soundtrack. An extended version of the *Adi Mantra* can be found on the accompanying soundtrack "*Yogable.*" Interestingly, when mantra is heard in recorded form it is more easily accepted by those who may be uneasy jumping into mantra *a cappella.* The recording can give the mantra credibility and make it user friendly by creating a sense of demystification.

PATTY (PATWANT) WILDASINN

Additional options for a non-traditional tune in can include the teacher mentally tuning in with *Ong Namo, Guru Dev Namo* prior to entering the facility, or doing so silently once seated in front of the class. If the entire group is not chanting together, it is still important to provide a time for the participants to transition peacefully into their yoga practice. This can be done by inviting students to close the eyes and take three slow, deep breaths in and out. Another option is to encourage students to take a few moments to close the eyes and mentally make a personal intention for their time on the yoga mat. These are simply suggestions. Feel free to be creative as you hold space and bring students, or yourself, into practice.

Ong Namo and here we go!

4

The Mindful Breath

"To master our breath is to be in control of our bodies and minds."
-Thich Nhat Hanh (2019)

What do we all do when we're stressed out, angry, or anxious? We breathe. What do we all do when we're joyous and happy? We breathe. What do we all do for the entirety of our lives while on this planet? We breathe. Unfortunately for many people, the vast majority of breathing is done unconsciously. The rate and intensity of the breath are fairly accurate indicators of one's emotional state. The breath is a powerful tool we can use to support and mold feelings of well-being – or not. So, the good news is that we can bring mindfulness to the breath in order to shift and uplift our mood and being. Breath work in yoga is called *pranayam,* and it refers to using the breath for fundamental energy management.

I've included a chapter on breathing in this book because I have found that many older students and special needs kids and adults have some difficulty identifying the flow of their breath and even distinguishing between the inhale and exhale. For some, it is difficult to breathe fully through the nose, while others tend to hold the breath without any awareness that they have stopped breathing. Breath is a topic to return to again and again with any special population.

In yoga philosophy, we say that the mind will follow the breath and the body will follow the mind. When we can stay in control and guide the breath consciously, we can maintain command of the mind, and thus the body. Basically, the breath is in charge.

In charge of what? you may ask. It is in charge of how we relate to and respond to our bodies, circumstances, and to the environment around us. We have the power to create our emotional states, or at a minimum to support them, simply by how we breathe. For example, a fast, shallow breath can foster panic or anger in the body and mind, whereas a slow, deep, steady breath can help to promote peace and serenity in the body and mind.

Proper breath is the foundation for life, the key to accessing both body and mind. Stress in our bodies can cause dysfunctional breathing patterns. Breath is life, but many people breathe in ways that are actually harmful to the body including shallow, erratic, fast rate, and upper chest breathing, leading to chronic tension and weakness. Holding tension and emotional trauma in the muscular system creates rigidity and an automatic protection response in the body. Proper breathing helps to release this rigidity and open the body to health, vitality, and increased concentration.

The typical adult breathes at a rate of sixteen-to-twenty cycles per minute. I have observed, however, that for many seniors new to yoga, the breath comes more quickly and is shallow in nature. They also may have a harder time with deep breathing and suspending the breath. Individuals with special needs often do not initially distinguish between the inhale and the exhale.

By consciously working with and slowing down the rate of breath, positive changes happen in the body and mind. For example, by slowing the breath rate down to eight cycles per minute, healing, stress relief, relaxation, and mental awareness are all increased. Slowing the breath down to four cycles per minute adds increased mental function and sensitivity to the list of benefits. This four-cycle breath can easily be done by inhaling for five seconds, suspending the breath for five seconds, and exhaling for five seconds, repeating the pattern for 3 to 5 minutes. Each breath should be complete and not rushed.

Let's try yogic breathing

A full yogic breath is helpful for creating calm and healing. This can be done comfortably sitting up or lying down with any population. (A fun and kid-friendly sponge breath will follow later in Chapter 9 Family Fun and Function.) Allow yourself to observe the breath coming in and out through the nose, without changing anything. Breathing through the nose is important because the air coming in is cleansed and hydrated through the nose. As you observe your breath, slowly bring your attention to your belly, and on the inhale bring the breath down to the navel and gently expand your belly. Release the breath, letting all of the air go. Make sure you exhale completely before taking a new, fresh and complete inhale. As you inhale again, slowly expand the belly, and bring the expansion up the fill the lower lobes of the lungs. Exhale completely. This time expand the breath even further, creating a three-part wave. Inhale, the wave begins to swell in your belly, draw it up expanding the lower lobes of the lungs, and bring it up throughout the lungs all the way up to the collarbone. Release the breath from the collarbone, down through the lungs, and lastly let the navel move gently toward the spine as all of the air is expelled. Continue inhaling and exhaling in this three-part wave for three to eleven minutes. If you are new to full yogic breathing and you begin to feel light-headed or dizzy, ease up a bit, as this may be a totally new approach to the breath. The breath should not be forced but allowed to flow.

This is a beautiful practice. And, it's just that – practice. When you take time to consciously practice breathing properly, you have the technique accessible to you when you're out in the perceived "real world." This practice is actually meditation. Today's typical yogis don't go around breathing with a full three-part yogic breath all day long, but rather know how to breathe properly, and have practiced. Practice creates the ability to call upon and use the breath to help take action in the world rather than reacting, helping us stay in command of the body.

For a further calming and balancing effect, you can try this full breath while breathing through the left nostril only. Again, sit or lie down comfortably, then plug the right nostril with the right thumb and begin inhaling and exhaling only through the left nostril. If you find that the left nostril is a little bit (or a lot) plugged up, just do the best you can. An ideal practice can range anywhere from 3 to 31 minutes of Long Deep Breathing through one or both nostrils.

An interesting yoga tidbit about the nostrils, as taught by Gurucharan Khalsa Ph.D., is that they automatically switch predominant sides approximately every 90 minutes, which affects the brain and our communication. With observation over time, you may notice that one of the nostrils is dominant, or remains open the majority of the time giving you input into the primary expression of your energy. To support and encourage balance in the brain we activate both nostrils.

The left nostril stimulates the feminine, cooling and calming energy, and the right nostril stimulates the masculine energy, warming and energizing the body. A radically simple explanation is that right-nostril predominance enhances alertness and focus, and left-nostril predominance enhances relaxation and even sleep. The breath and our body are full of little secrets that when uncovered can assist us in reaching our desired or full potential.

Listen to your breath. The deeper the breath, the better the emotional regulation it brings. The slower the breath, the better clarity it brings.

The bottom line is that breath is obviously essential for life, but mindful, conscious breath can also improve the quality of our lives. Proper breath contributes to increased well-being, balance, and stability in the body and mind. Breath is the basis for a yoga practice. The breath is all you have every moment – be present! Open yourself to the powerful possibility of your breath.

BREATHE
The Poetry of Michael

I've replaced belief,
with the experience of living...
Both Grace and I had met at
the top of the mountain
and It was there
through the soul
that an endlessness
would birth an eternal
knowing...
My relationship with the
unknown
would melt the pain
felt and carried
by the young boy
who once was cast
at the center of the sea
chained by fear-
into a methodical dance,
where both eternity
and I,
would fade
back into one...
So why wait for a symphony to
lead you into the sky,
when you can become the music,
that breathes new life...
For the resurrection of truth
is to become you...
it is there
that you shall become the stars,
become the poem,
and as they read you
walk through life-
Know,
that you hold the key.
to a deathless life...
Now,
become the night

breathe as the night;
breathe until you become the
light of day…
Breathe hope into the heart,
that has become an apsis
to the body,
and an abyss
for the dark…
Breathe,
and face yourself…
Allow yourself to feel the depth of pain
that lives inside of you…
Breathe until you no longer
fear death;
Breathe until both death and
life become a
myth,
a story actualizing itself
through
the narration,
of immeasurability…
Breathe until
you feel the echo
of the unending pulse
descend back into
being…
Breathe until the only thing that
Is left,
Is love…

A note from the poet, Michael Mejia (unpub. ms.):

"Through synchronicity, Kundalini Yoga would enter my life in one of my darkest hours. After surviving a near fatal head injury, I would undergo a spontaneous kundalini awakening. I didn't have a reference point for the energetic symptoms I was suffering from, through divine intervention – I was led to Kundalini Yoga. The practice brought balance, hope and healing. After enduring ten years of writer's block each energetic initiation would create a space for the poetry that lived in my soul – to move back into the heart.

As energy continues to move through my body's centers and create clear pathways for prana to advance freely, Kundalini Yoga has served as an invisible bridge between the worlds of form and formless."

5

Cushions, Chairs, and Choices

Warm Ups, Posture Modification, and Basic Mudra

"How can I judge anything – knowing that I am everything."
- The Poetry of Michael (2020)

This chapter gives descriptions for wonderful warm-up exercise options, exercises to stretch and open the flow of energy to the spine, hips, legs, shoulders, the whole body. Although warm-ups are not a required element of yoga, they can be quite beneficial in preparing for a yoga *kriya*, (a complete set or sequence of exercises) allowing the body to not only stretch, but also settle into a seated posture offering increased comfort and a sense of grounding. They are after all actual yoga postures, and putting a series of warm-ups together can provide a gentle practice in itself.

Typically, only a few warm-ups are suggested prior to practicing a *kriya*. However, in gentle yoga I have found increasing the number of warm-ups can assist in creating a more comfortable and safe practice. Taking time with thorough attention to the body, helping to move beyond tightness, tension and minor aches and pains is effective in achieving the best results.

The choice of warm-ups can be determined by what the body needs at any given time. Another simple idea is to take a look at the *kriya* and practice warm-up exercises that differ from what is in the *kriya* for a complementary full body approach. For instance, if there is a lot of sitting in the exercise set, pick warm-ups that stretch the legs and hips, or get up on the feet to move. If the set has many standing postures, choose seated warm-ups such as Spinal Flex or Pelvic Rotation. Allow for flexibility in body, mind and planning.

The following are exercises that can be used as warm-ups for the effect of getting the body ready to practice yoga. If you don't have time for a full yoga practice you can add a few of these recommended postures to any exercise routine you may already have, or practice a few postures anytime throughout the day to stretch and reboot. Each warm-up can be practiced for 1 to 3 minutes. Although some of these postures are found and illustrated in the *kriyas* recommended in this book, I am taking care here to provide a more complete explanation, along with benefits of the movement. The pace of warm-ups can be slow and easy, or intensity of movement and breath may be individualized for each student. Most of the typical seated movements can be done while sitting on the floor, in a chair, or even while standing.

Seated Warm-ups:

The following exercises can be done in a chair as well as on the floor. Easy Pose can be alternated with Rock Pose (sitting on the heels), extending the legs out in front of the body, or even Butterfly Pose, bringing the bottom of the feet together as knees fall open to each side. The use of yoga blocks or folded blankets under the thighs or knees in a crossed leg pose, such as in Easy Pose, helps to support the legs and hips and takes pressure off the joints. Sitting on a folded blanket may also ease the joints, as the small lift it creates helps to release the hips. Feel free to utilize a blanket or blocks for aid in any seated posture. [1]

If using a yoga block for support in posture, I recommend using a foam block that is firm with a bit of give when squeezed. Cork or wood blocks may be too hard and uncomfortable for the suggested block uses herein. Block placement should provide comfortable support. A blanket can be lain over a block for additional comfort.

If using a chair for yoga practice, it is important to sit up tall with the spine slightly away from the back of the chair, and the feet flat on the floor. Scoot toward the edge of the chair to ground the feet on the floor, with the knees bent at a ninety-degree angle. If the feet do not reach the floor, put a yoga block on the ground and place the feet on the block. The knees should be in alignment with the ankles, not bent out extending over the feet. Scooting forward in the chair does not mean balancing precariously at the edge. Move forward enough so that the back is not touching the chair, but the chair is still grounded on the floor and the body is fully supported by the chair.

Pelvic Rotation – Sit in Easy Pose, hold on to the knees and rotate the torso on the pelvis moving the spine in a big circle. Find your own range of motion to make it gentle and move with the breath; inhale and exhale with each rotation. Move in each direction for equal amounts of time.

---

[1] The illustrations are true to the author's vision. They are simple and sweet, and give a general guide for the position and movement in each posture. It is recommended that the reader review the written descriptions included with the given exercises, postures, and meditations for specific details.

PATTY (PATWANT) WILDASINN

This posture opens energy at the base of the spine, works on flexibility of the spine, and is good for the liver and the digestive tract.

Spinal Flex – Sit in Easy Pose, hold on to the ankles, while you inhale rock the pelvis forward stretching the chest forward, then exhale as you rock the pelvis back while rounding the lower back. For a gentle modification, the movement can be made slower and smaller as needed. The chin remains fairly level to the floor, and we do not flip-flop the head in this Spinal Flex. We're not bobble head figurines. All versions of Spinal Flex work on increasing flexibility in the spine, circulating spinal fluid, and increasing focus, concentration, and memory. Varying versions of this flex give slight changes to the position of hands and legs and help to target different areas along the spinal column, shifting the range of motion.

Spinal Twist – Sit in Easy Pose and hold on to the shoulders, fingers in front, thumbs in back, and begin to twist from side to side. Inhale as you move left and exhale as you move right. The head and neck move only as they are attached to the spine, not independently. For a gentle version, if the hands do not reach the shoulders, you may need to bring the arms in front of the body with hands in fists directly in front of the shoulders and move slowly. Spinal Twist is good for the spine, liver, heart center, and waistline.

Spinal Lean - Sit in Easy Pose, hands on shoulders (or in fists as described for spinal twist). Lean gently from side to side, inhaling as you move left and exhaling as you move right. As one elbow moves down to one side, the opposite elbow reaches up toward the sky. This works on the spine, the magnetic field, and is good for the waistline.

Shoulder Rolls – Sit in Easy Pose with the hands resting on knees or thighs. Begin rolling the shoulders in a backward direction, inhaling as the shoulders move up and exhaling as they move down. Switch directions, rolling the shoulders forward as you follow the same breathing pattern, inhaling up and exhaling down. Practice an equal length of time in each direction. Shoulder rolls massage the lungs, release stress and tension, and begin to loosen the neck area, increasing circulation to the head.

Neck Rolls – Sit up tall in Easy Pose and lengthen the spine. Tilt the chin to the chest and begin to rotate the head in a circle stretching the neck as you rotate. Move with the breath, inhale as the head comes around the back and exhale as the head moves around in front. This exercise can be made very gentle by making the movement small and slow. Switch directions and practice for the same length of time. Another option for those with cervical spine issues is to tilt the chin down and slowly move the chin toward one shoulder and then the other in a semi-circle movement in front of the body. Neck rolls help to release stress, tension and tightness, as well as stimulate the higher glands in the body.

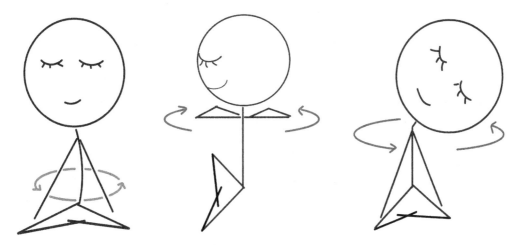

Forward Folds:

The next trio of exercises are versions of the Life Nerve Stretch, which is basically a forward fold. When we move into forward folds it provides a great opportunity to watch and feel the breath. When folding forward, feel the breath moving down the spine into the lower back with each inhale and then back up the spine as the breath is released. Open the lower back and deepen the stretch with the use of the breath. Think of taking a wide inhale and a tall exhale, as you expand and release. It is important to keep a steady flow of the breath during the forward fold whether it be long, slow, deep, powerful, or Breath of Fire.

A yoga strap is a great way to reach the feet while in a forward fold position. Simply put the strap around the bottoms of both feet, toward the balls of the feet, and take one end of the strap in each hand. From here, adjust the straps as needed to come into a forward fold. The straps are merely an extension of the arms that provide both support and resistance. The use of a strap in this stretch enables students to ease up on the lower back so as not to strain and contort as they fold forward. The idea is to provide support and resistance, not necessarily to push further into the stretch. Overdoing work with a yoga strap can cause injury, so straps and other props must be used with intention and moderation. Forward folds stretch the back of the legs, the lower back, and allow for increased circulation into the torso.

Life Nerve Stretch, Both Legs- Sit up tall and extend the legs out in front of you flat on the floor, keeping a few inches of space between your feet. Inhale as you stretch up from the base of the spine and lift the hands overhead, then exhale as you hinge forward from the hips, letting the belly come down first, then let the arms float down to hold on to toes, ankles, shins, knees, wherever you can reach, making sure that the legs remain straight. Let the head and neck relax down last and breathe long and deep – you may even add Breath of Fire!

<u>Life Nerve Stretch Left and Right</u> – Follow the instructions for Life Nerve Stretch, extending the left leg out in front of you, while bending the right knee and bringing the right foot to the left thigh. Fold forward, then switch sides.

<u>Life Nerve Stretch with Wide Legs</u> – Sit with the legs forward and spread the feet out as wide as comfortable; legs are straight. Keep the knees and the toes pointing up toward the ceiling to avoid collapsing the legs in either direction and to protect the joints of the legs. Lengthen the spine, and bend forward and hold the toes, ankles, shins, or above the knees. Commit to the hold creating a circuit with the flow of energy. Inhale up to the center, then exhale down to the left side; inhale up, then exhale down to the right and repeat with a powerful breath. Make sure to find the right fit for your reach and breath intensity, making sure not to over-extend the distance between the legs. This movement can be fast and powerful or slow and gentle. An alternate posture is to move straight up and down with the breath, or to fold straight forward and hold the stretch stationary with long deep breathing.

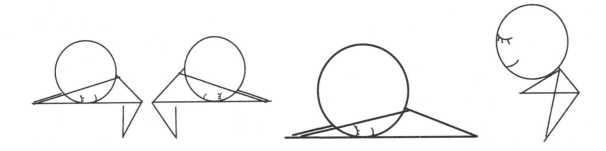

Standing warm-ups:

Standing warm-ups provide a targeted stretch and stimulate balance in the body and brain. Feet are positioned as a foundation to support your base balance.

<u>Miracle Bends</u> – Affectionately named because this forward fold works the entire spine. Stand up with feet hip distance. Inhale with both arms up over the head, exhale and fold forward bringing the hands down toward the ground. The hands may reach for the knees as an alternative to the ground. The inhale can be done with the spine and arms lifting straight up, or with a slight backward reach into an easy backbend. Continue inhaling up and exhaling down in the Miracle Bend.

<u>Standing Spinal Twist</u> – Stand with the feet slightly wider than the hips and twist from side to side. The arms are stretched out straight to the sides, with elbows bent to 90 degrees, hands up in *Gyan Mudra*, or alternately with the hands on the shoulders as in a seated spinal twist. There is a blissful version of twisting to the left while extending the left arm and then bending the right elbow bringing the right hand into the heart center on the inhale, then exhale and switch the arms. Bless yourself at the heart center while twisting.

Standing Spinal Lean – Stand with the feet hip width apart, arms loose at the sides, and begin to lean from side to side, inhaling left and exhaling right.

Hammer Circle – Take a wide stance and lift the arms up overhead, so that they remain loose without tension. Inhale at the top, then swing down to the left and exhale, coming up all the way around to the right until you end up where you started. Switch directions as you swing down and around and back up. Inhale when the arms are up, exhale as they sweep down in front of you. I liken this to the loose flexibility of a rag doll. Today's kids may have not even heard of rag dolls.

Wide Standing Bend – Take a wide balanced stance. Inhale arms up, exhale fold forward. The hands may rest on the ground, or on a block between the feet.

Rock on the Feet – Stand with the feet under the hips and begin to rock back and forth on the feet, up on to the balls and toes, then back onto the heels. Excellent for balance, which is a considerable concern for aging populations.

Single Leg Balance- Stand on one leg and extend the other behind as you lift it off the floor, while the opposite arm extends straight out in front of you. Switch sides.

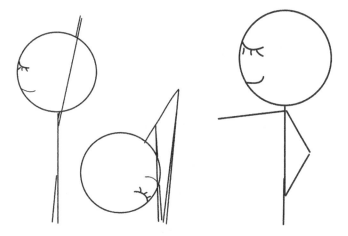

Warm-ups on hands and knees:

Working on the hands and knees may not be comfortable for those with tender wrists or past injuries. If this is the case, bring the hands into fists and place the knuckles down on the ground to stabilize the wrists. If this does not alleviate discomfort, drop down onto the elbows, or forego postures on the hands and knees altogether.

Cat-Cow – Come on to the hands and knees, hands under the shoulders and knees under the hips and begin to flex the spine. Inhale into Cow Pose with the head up, bottom up, belly down, and exhale into Cat Pose by arching the spine up, tucking the tail bone, and dropping the head. Cat-Cow is sometimes referred to as the self-chiropractor, and is excellent for supporting circulation, flexibility and alignment of the spine. Two fists placed on the floor between the knees bring the knees into alignment with the hips. It's a little trick to gauge that the knees are actually placed at hip distance.

Balance on Hands and Knees – On the hands and knees, extend the right leg straight back behind and the left arm straight out in front palm down, hold for up to 1 minute, then switch sides. Engage the core and find a focal point to help with balance. Hands and feet may be flexed or slightly pointed in this posture. Choose one or the other so it's congruent. This posture has the added benefit of a cross-crawl exercise in that it stimulates balance in the body and the brain.

Circle the Hips - On the hands and knees, with a neutral spine and the head relaxed down, begin to rotate the hips in large circles, stretching in each direction of the circle. Switch directions of the rotation for an equal length of time.

Warm-ups lying on the back:

Legs up the Wall- Works to release tight neck muscles and prevent headaches. Lie on the floor with your bottom against the wall and extend the legs up along the wall. Start with the feet in alignment with the hips and adjust the width of the legs for comfort. The wall provides support for the legs and back, and can assist with stretching the life nerve. Move the bottom away from the wall to decrease the intensity of the stretch.

Alternate Leg Lifts – Lie on the back with the palms facing down next to the hips, or tucked under the hips to provide additional support for the lower back. Begin lifting one leg up to ninety degrees then back down, alternating sides. Inhale up and exhale down. This can be a friendly alternative to double leg lifts found in any yoga set to take strain off the lower back. As an additional option, alternate legs may be brought into the chest with bent knees, and held for a few breaths each.

Cat Stretch - Lie on the back and bring one knee in toward the chest. Reach across the body and take the knee in the opposite hand, drawing it across the body. Extend the other arm out along the floor and try to keep both shoulders grounded. Switch sides. This provides a twist for the spine, a stretch for the hips, and an opening of the shoulders. In addition, this posture creates a spiral energy along the spinal column that helps to balance the magnetic field. This stretch is recommended when coming out of deep relaxation. An alternate posture is to lie on the back and extend the arms out along the ground, bent knees, and feet on the floor at hip distance. From here twist the spine while guiding bent knees to one side of the body and the other, like windshield wipers.

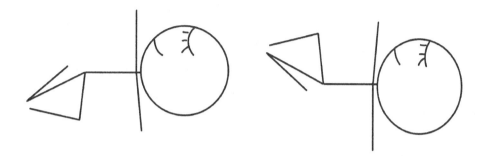

Cross-Crawl warm-ups:

This particular group of exercises are extremely beneficial for the brain as well as the body. For simplicity I refer to all exercises that simultaneously use the opposite sides of the body; hands, arms, feet, and legs cross-crawl movements. Some of these movements will cross the body at the midline (vertical center of the body) boosting the positive effect on the brain. Cross-crawl exercises can be done standing, sitting, or lying on the ground.

Basic March with Arm Lifts – Stand with the feet under the hips and get ready to move. Inhale and lift the left knee up into a march while raising the right arm up over the head, then exhale, releasing them down. Switch sides and continue alternating. This can be practiced more gently by slowing it down into a walking motion. Lifting the knees into a high march is good for the cardiovascular system. This posture may also be practiced by lying on the back as you bring one knee into the chest and the opposite arm up over the head onto the floor.

March and Cross Arms – Begin a marching or walking movement. Then add arms by crossing one across the body to touch the opposite knee when it is in the upward position. Switch sides, and continue touching opposite hands and knees.

Behind Body Cross-Crawl – Stand on the feet and begin alternately lifting the feet up behind and across the body. Try to reach behind with the opposite hand and tap the foot as it lifts off the ground. In this version, crossing the midline happens in back of the body. The feet and hands may or may not reach to touch.

Windmills – (These take me back to Junior High, every time.) Stand with the legs wide, arms out to the sides parallel to the floor. Inhale in this position, exhale and fold down to the side reaching the left hand toward the right foot or knee, then inhale back to the start position and switch sides. This posture may also be done in a wide leg seated position. This exercise is good for the bowel system, as well as flexibility.

Criss-Cross Legs – The legs can be moved in a criss-cross pattern while jumping. Jump the feet apart to each side, and then cross the feet with each jump back in, alternating which foot crosses in front on each repetition. Or, take it down a notch and walk through the motion without the jump. This criss-cross pattern with the legs may also be practiced while lying on the back on the ground. Elevate the legs off the ground to an angle that can be held comfortably and scissor, legs wide on the inhale and cross on the exhale. The legs may cross at the ankles or the knees. The angle of the legs may range from ninety degrees, straight up toward the ceiling, to only six inches off the floor adjusting for personal comfort level. The lower the legs, the harder the abdominals work, and legs at a higher angle are easier on the lower back.

Criss-Cross Arms – Extend the arms straight out from the shoulders in front of the body. Inhale in this position, exhale and cross the arms in front of the body and repeat, alternating the cross of the arms with each repetition. The range of motion in the arms may be small or large, just make sure they cross the center of the body with each exhale.

Mudras/Hand Positions and Bandhas/Body Locks

Gyan Mudra
Gyan Mudra is a frequently indicated mudra, or hand position, and is found in the *kriyas* contained in this book. To practice *Gyan Mudra*, bring the tips of the index fingers to touch the tips of the thumbs. This is sometimes called the seal of life. You are creating a seal between the finger tips, applying a firm, but not hard, pressure. The index finger is the Jupiter finger and ties into knowledge and wisdom. Bringing these fingertips together stimulates inner wisdom and knowledge.

Venus Lock

Venus Lock is also used in the yoga in this book. Venus Lock is an interlacing of the fingers, bringing the hands together. Traditionally it was taught that women interlace with the left thumb on top, so that it is in the outermost position, and men interlace in the opposite way, with the right thumb on the outside. Left stimulates the feminine energy, which is cooling and calming, and the right stimulates the masculine energy, which is warming and energizing. It is appropriate to encourage each student to choose their Venus Lock based on whether they want to work with the Divine Feminine energy or the Divine Masculine energy based on current needs and mood.

Toe Lock

Although technically not a lock, the toe hold used in forward folds is a technique that is sometimes referred to as the toe lock. If the seated forward fold affords the opportunity to reach the toes, it is recommended to take the index and middle finger and wrap them around the back of the big toe, while gently pressing on the toenail with the thumb. The ring finger and pinky tuck in toward the palm. This gentle pressure point provides a grounding point for the fold and stimulates the pituitary gland.

Mulbandh

The *Mulbandh* or Root Lock can be used in a variety of yoga postures. It can be applied on a suspended inhale or exhale. The Root Lock is applied by contracting the muscles of the rectum, sex organs and navel point with a gentle upward pull. Energy is directed up along the spinal column for integration. This moves in line with the natural flow of energy in the body.

Applying a gentle Root Lock will help to create a stable internal foundation for most seated postures, especially during meditation. This gentle, or light pull of the Root Lock also helps provide support for the spine and improves the overall posture of the body.

Jalandhar Bandh

Jalandhar Bandh or Neck Lock is typically applied when the spine is straight, as in a seated posture. The Neck Lock is applied by simultaneously lengthening the back of the neck and pulling the chin slightly in and back, but not up and down. The head stays in a neutral position and the chest remains up and open. This lock provides focus, stabilization, and proper flow both physically and energetically between the head and the body.

Body locks work much like breath in the sense that they are tools for energy management.

Two more locks that are not found in the practices contained in this book, but that are worth mentioning, are *Uddiyana Bandh* which is the Diaphragm Lock and *Maha Bandh* which refers to applying all the body locks at the same time to create the Great Lock.

Classic Yoga Posture and Modifications

The world of yoga is vast. However, different branches of yoga do share 108 basic postures and the variations thereof. The *kriyas* included in this book come from the practice of Kundalini yoga. Modifications have been given alongside the original teachings in order to give the practitioner choices to suit the individual student bodies. Kundalini yoga is not typically taught with the use of props, and the instructors do not give hands-on physical adjustments, only verbal cues to proper alignment. The idea behind this is for the practitioner to be in a posture that their body is able to hold while maintaining the correct angles and triangles. Moreover, this book does give some alternate supportive positions using props such as blocks, blankets, and straps.

If there is any posture, even with modifications, that induces pain or does not feel right, the solution is to abstain from that pose. Instead, mentally visualize the posture and breathe.

Testimonials:

"Several years ago, I became deathly ill with Hashimoto's thyroiditis and Chronic Fatigue. Regardless of what I did, relief was not obtained. A friend suggested I take yoga lessons. In my efforts to feel better, I looked for a nearby studio, and found yoga. I committed to twice a week and the commitment quickly became a daily ritual. There were many poses I couldn't hold, sitting in 'Easy Pose' was painful and meditating for three minutes would cause anxiety. However, with time I learned how to breathe, I learned that holding a pose is not critical; imagining the pose holds the same effect. There were set back days and being present was a maximum effort. During those times I learned that envisioning the asanas had a tremendous effect. The community of yogis, the energy in the room, the good vibrations carried me in my practice. With time sitting in Easy Pose became second nature and position of choice.

Wherever I was in my practice, it was perfect for me. Modifications were made from easy to stretching myself to create the maximum benefit and contour for flexibility or lack of, for each particular day. In my practice there could be one morning that a pose done with ease for years is difficult. The modifications allow to gradually return to my level of competence. Sometimes the process takes minutes, but it can take a day, days or months. Having options enables you to continue.

When I found myself on the road to recovery, I became a yoga instructor and now help others on their healing journey."

- Dr. G.

"I like instructions that are clear and easy to follow, modifications, and the encouragement to listen to my own body. The environment is warm with great camaraderie, always fun, light hearted and enlightening. I always leave class with a smile and a greater sense of wellbeing."

- Steve W.

"My physical, emotional, and spiritual experience with kundalini yoga has been a source of peace and strength in all areas of my life – teaching, parenting, partnering, growing as a person. It has helped me cope with the challenges of aging and disability. A text on yoga for special needs people is much needed and will be very welcome."

-Dr. DD W.

6

Gentle Yoga; Be Kind and Move

"There is no perfect posture, only your posture. Nothing more is asked
than to be who you are. And then…be open to surprises."
– Gurucharan Singh Khalsa, Ph.D. (2018)

Why a Gentle Approach to Yoga?

The body is an amazing vessel capable of renewing, healing, and recovery. The body is our teacher, our tour guide, our only vehicle for experiencing life on this planet. We have energetic bodies that play out their parts in and around the physical body, but the physical body is the vessel. As long as there is breath in the body, we have an opportunity to change, grow, and take steps to create the life we desire.

How many of us can say we embrace and love our bodies just as they are in the present moment? How about in all present moments? Did you smile and say, "I do!" or did you snort in derision?

I snorted, then I smiled.

How many of us can say we've ever experienced a feeling of body betrayal? Maybe the body doesn't look like it used to, doesn't do what it used to, or move in the way that we want. Changes may seem beyond our control. At times, when the mind as well as the body don't behave as we want them to, we may begin to feel overwhelmed or even powerless. If this happens often enough and for long enough, we begin to reject and deny the body we were given, possibly on a level that's beyond our own awareness.

In yogic tradition, the body is viewed as a temple, and we are encouraged to take care of it as such. I can assure you that this concept does not come naturally or easily for many people. It can be especially hard to connect with the impulse to make the effort to take care of a body that feels as if it is betraying us.

From a yoga perspective, there are ways to gently and effectively support the body, self-acceptance, and personal growth in the present moment.

The present moment is a key concept. So, first things first, allow the self to be here now. Yes, give yourself permission to be in the present moment. I stress the idea of being in the now because, as humans, many of us spend the vast majority of our time in the past or the future, ruminating over what we cannot change from the past, or projecting expectations into the future.

All of life - healing, loving, grieving, laughing, hurting - all living takes place in the present moment.

Be here now, move, and listen. Listen to the innocence of your heartbeat. The heart has its own intelligence, and is a far better guide than the head. Yoga helps to bring the heart and the head into alignment. Listen to your body as you connect with the heart and the breath. Move into the wisdom of the heart.

What are students looking for in a Gentle Yoga class?

Students come seeking a place where they will not be judged. I find they want to give gentle yoga a try to keep the body moving and to maintain or improve their health. Students have reported seeking out gentle yoga as a means of finding flexibility and stress relief, to reduce inflammation, to exercise and promote relaxation, all in a place where they can work at their own pace. Many end up in a gentle class when they find that their physical abilities have become more limited than they once were. Others are looking for a spiritual component, a practice with multiple layers, and a place where all religions, philosophies and ideas are welcomed. Yoga definitely fits this bill, but what new students may be surprised to find is how the subtle energetic shifts in mood and mind are experienced to support the entire being.

The best description I've ever heard in one of my yoga classes came from a new student. After her first class, she came up to me and said, *"That was really weird…. but I feel really good."* I replied, *"That's the point!"* The practice of Kundalini is not a look good yoga, it's a feel good yoga.

What do we do to be gentle?

We practice the yoga, deliver the yoga teachings, and incorporate modifications as they are appropriate for the individual level of physical fitness and flexibility, taking into account any past injuries, surgeries, or current issues. In the recommended yoga sets that are given in this and the following chapters, both the full, original set will be given, along with suggestions by the author for adaptations when and if needed.

From years of experience, I would like to make clear that the suggestions I share for modifications are *"more like guidelines than actual rules."* (Yes, that was said in my head in the voice of Geoffrey Rush playing Captain Barbosa in Disney's *Pirates of the Caribbean, Curse of the Black Pearl*, and yes, I say it out loud that way when I teach a class.) Breathe in deep and embrace the mutiny of free will and personal choice. By embracing mutiny I'm suggesting to be a bit of a rule breaker as you let go of the idea of perfection and choose a yoga practice to suit your body.

All goofiness aside, please know that a gentle class does not necessarily translate as easy. But, having fun is encouraged.

The typical class outline observed for a Kundalini Yoga class is as follows:
Tune in with *Ong Namo, Guru Dev Namo* (You may also use an alternate choice, as outlined in Chapter 3.)
Warm-ups (Warm-ups are optional, but useful in a gentle practice as outlined in Chapter 5.)
Kriya (yoga set)
Deep Relaxation
Meditation
Sat Nam

One of the first challenges to face in the physical practice of Gentle Yoga may be the 'dreaded' Easy Pose. For many gentle yoga students, Easy Pose is a contradiction, a paradox if you will, and one of the most uncomfortable parts of yoga practice. I have a student who actually calls it "*hard pose.*" One of the first things you need to do is find a comfortable, or at least semi-comfortable, easy seat. I invite you to move and adjust your legs as needed. A comfortable Easy Pose may be achieved by placing cushions or blankets under the buttocks to take some of the pressure off knee and hip joints, or under the thighs and knees for support. You may alternate extending and stretching your legs out in front of you if you wish, or even extend them out together. Some may find their easy seat in a wide Butterfly Pose or even seated in a chair.

Keep Up with *Ahimsa*

The motto of the Aquarian Age is "*Keep Up!*"

Before moving forward with posture or breath work, I'd like to introduce you to the concept of "keeping up" with the spirit of *ahimsa. Ahimsa* (which translates as "non-harming") is one of the Eight Limbs of Yoga, specifically one of the *yamas,* or intentional restraints in behavior and attitude. I invite you to approach yoga with the principle of *ahimsa,* practicing love and compassion for self and others without causing harm.

"Keeping up can include beginning again!"
- Gurucharan Singh Khalsa, Ph.D. (personal communication)

Pay attention and be aware of how you feel while in a posture and make adjustments as necessary. If you find it a struggle to sit, get up on your feet as you move the body into warm-ups. The pace for warm-ups can be slowed down for gentle yoga. Many of the typical seated postures may be done while sitting on the floor, in a chair, or even standing. When modifying a *kriya,* often it is appropriate to proportionately shorten the times. For instance, providing a gentle experience, it may be that one minute of each posture is practiced instead of 3 minutes, along with any needed modifications. Times can be built up to full recommendations slowly with practice.

It is best to practice yoga with your feet bare and your stomach empty, or at least not full. It is fine to sip water during your yoga session.

What is a *Kriya*?

A *kriya* is a sequence of prescribed yoga postures or an exercise set which may also include breath work and meditation. It is considered a complete action. The Kundalini *kriyas* herein are given as originally taught by Yogi Bhajan. I have included additional notes and options for making postures more accessible to a gentle practice.

Recommended *Kriyas*: (Found at the end of the chapter.)
I have picked these yoga sets intentionally, even though some include challenging postures, in order to demonstrate how you can practice any type of yoga *kriya* in a gentle way.
Kriya for Elevation
Kriya to Strengthen the Aura
Kriya for Pelvic Balance

Upon concluding a *kriya,* there is typically a period of deep relaxation (*savasana*) practiced while lying on the back to allow for the assimilation of the yoga prior to meditation. Relaxation can last anywhere from 3 to 11 minutes. I personally recommend 6 to 7 minutes of relaxation for a gentle class. Sometimes the meditation is included in the *kriya*, and deep relaxation follows, otherwise meditation is typically practiced after relaxation. (A multitude of Kundalini *kriyas* can be found in the numerous Kundalini yoga manuals in publication. I am outlining only a few in this book.) Wherever deep relaxation may fall in the structure of the practice it is important to find a comfortable posture, typically lying on the back with the arms and legs away from the torso, palms facing up with relaxed fingers, and feet dropping slightly out to the side. This may also be called Corpse Pose. Any discomfort experienced in the lower back while the legs are extended along the ground may be alleviated by bending the knees and keeping the feet flat on the floor. A further release in the lower back may be achieved by dropping the bent knees toward the midline of the body so that the insides of the knees touch while relaxing. Upon exiting the period of *savasana* a wake-up routine is helpful in coming back to awareness and the physical body, providing movement in a way that allows one to come back to the present slowly and safely. Begin by bringing awareness back to the body and breath, then wiggle the fingers and toes, rotate the wrists and ankles, take a cat-stretch to each side (found in chapter 5), rub the palms and the bottoms of the feet together, and lastly bring the knees into the chest and rock the body up and down on the spine a few times before rocking all the way back up into Easy Pose.

When waking up from deep relaxation in a gentle way, the aforementioned routine is followed. When it comes to the end and the knees are drawn in toward the chest with the arms holding them in place, I suggest rocking side to side to massage the lower back against the ground before rocking up and down along the spine to sit up. Another option that can be helpful is to roll all the way over to one side and use the arms to assist in bringing the body back up to a seated posture. This may be especially helpful for those with back issues, vertigo, or those prone to dizziness. The most important thing is to come from a prone position up to a seated posture without stressing or hurting the lower back. This holds true for very gentle yoga as well, which is found in the next chapter.

Meditation is a crucial part of the practice of yoga, and I outline close to a dozen specific meditation practices in this book. Meditation helps to develop a neutral mind (also called the meditative mind), focus, concentration, awareness, clarity, calming, stability and an overall sense of well-being. For proper rhythm and pronunciation many of the meditations with mantra given in this book can be found on soundtrack titled "*Yogable*" by Jap Dharam Rose. The link for purchase is included with mantras found at the end of the book.

Upon the conclusion of a yoga class or personal practice, we recite a saying called *The Long Time Sun*. (This saying is found in more detail in Chapter 8.) Chanting a *Sat Nam* is the final end of a session, which provides closure with reverence and a sense of grounding. The *Sat* is a long vibration, followed by a short, soft *Nam*. *Sat Nam* is a mantra to honor truth as identity for all. *Namaste* would be the familiar closing mantra for a Hatha practice, honoring the spirit in all. Both of these mantras are typically accompanied by a seated forward bow.

Recommended meditations: (Found at the end of the chapter.)
Kirtan Kriya
Anti-Hypertension Meditation
At Wits End, or Meditation for When You Don't Know What to do

If you are a yoga teacher, it is important not to impose self-perceived limitations by thinking, *"Oh, Gentle Yoga students can't do that! I better not teach that set!"* The same holds true for a personal practice, *"I can't do yoga because I'm not flexible. I can't do that."* Variations and choices are your friends. I'm not suggesting to change the *kriyas*, but offer them with adaptation while honoring the original thread. In gentle yoga, the emphasis is on experience, not so much precise alignment of posture. I would also like to add that gentle is all about perspective: it is subjective. Not everyone is going to be on the same page. That's the beauty of choices.

If rest is needed during a particular *asana* (posture), simply imagine being in the posture instead. In yoga we are always participating with the breath!

What about Breath of Fire in Gentle Yoga?

Yes! Yes! A resounding yes!

I like to share a story about my sister, whom I love dearly, to help boost confidence and morale in my gentle classes. Although my sister and I come from the same genetic background, we are intrinsically different in body and in mind. Whereas she can hang out in Cobra Pose comfortably for extended periods of time, me not so much. In turn, I can maintain Crow Pose comfortably, while that posture challenges her. No judgement is assigned; we all have unique strengths. So, at the expense of a good sister story, my students get to laugh and feel powerful. On occasion when I teach Breath of Fire and class participants are actively engaged, I share with them that my sister, "Miss Hot Power Yoga," says she doesn't practice Kundalini Yoga because "Breath of Fire is too hard" (said in a whining voice). It can take some time to get the hang of it, but once it clicks, Breath of Fire provides focus, determination, and can actually help in maintaining yoga posture. Outlined below are the mechanics and a list of general benefits of practicing Breath of Fire.

Breath of Fire

Breath of Fire is a rapid breath that closely resembles the panting of a dog. However, it is typically done through the nose. The breath is moved by a pumping or pulsing movement of the navel and solar plexus area. The diaphragm remains relaxed as it moves with the breath. On the inhale the belly is relaxed, and on the exhale the navel point/solar plexus contracts, pulling in toward the spine, pressing the diaphragm up so that all of the air is expelled from the lungs. The inhale and exhale are equal in duration; if you focus on the exhale, however, the inhale will take care of itself because your body wants to breathe. Breath of Fire is a diaphragmatic breath. Breath of Fire is fast and powerful, cleansing and energizing, and it does build heat within the body. Start slowly at 40 to 60 breaths per minute. The breath can be built up to 2-3 breaths per second.

Of course, Breath of Fire can be done at a slower pace, so if you start to feel dizzy take a break and return to a natural breath. I invite new students to place one hand on the belly to be sure that the contraction happens on the exhale as the body becomes accustomed to the practice of Breath of Fire. While this practice may feel awkward at first, it will soon become second nature.

It is interesting to note that some traditions refer to this practice as skull cleansing breath.

Benefits of Breath of Fire
- Oxygenates and purifies the body
- Releases toxins and deposits from the lungs, mucous linings, and blood vessels
- Expands lung capacity and increases vital strength
- Strengthens the entire nervous system, all seventy-two thousand nerves
- Restores balance between the sympathetic and parasympathetic nervous systems

- Strengthens the navel
- Increases physical endurance and prepares one to act effectively
- Helps to reduce addictive tendencies, thoughts, and impulses
- Promotes a positive neutrality in the mind
- Increases oxygen delivery to the brain
- Boosts immune system function
- Insulates the nerves, providing for a type of life force cushion
- Calms the disposition and combats stress

And my personal favorite -

- With regular practice, Breath of Fire can help to end embarrassing temper tantrum problems (you probably know someone you'd like to recommend this to!)

Breath of Fire is contraindicated for those who are:
- women in the first few days of their menstrual cycle
- experiencing diaphragm or rib injuries
- currently experiencing or are predisposed to pelvic organ prolapse
- pregnant
- experiencing pain with the breath
- children

As Breath of Fire is not typically appropriate for children, the rule of thumb I use is that students be at least sixteen years old before engaging in this practice. I choose this age because most have gone through puberty by this time. There are varied recommendations in yogic teachings as to guidelines for young people practicing a gentle Breath of Fire, but for safety and an abundance of caution I publicly recommend practicing this breath after the age of 16.

Reported Benefits and Testimonials:
- Increased overall flexibility
- Reduced levels of pain
- The practice is an unfolding journey
- The application of loving kindness in life
- Enhanced/deeper meditation states
- Found blessings and gratitude
- Uplifted spirit and open heart
- Less guilt
- Sense of community/new friends
- Reduced stress
- Healthy exercise
- Better eating habits
- Weight loss

- Increased energy
- Increased confidence

"Gentle yoga means that I can 'show up and keep up' in spite of bilateral hip replacements and allergy/asthma challenges. Instead of saying 'I can't' the modifications in a gentle class allow me to participate fully in the kriya and meditation thereby realizing the wonderful benefits of the Kundalini technology. There is no judgement in a gentle class as I move slowly and with a smaller range of motion. As my body continues to change with the coming years, I know my practice will not be interrupted."

– Areta H.

"A friend shared the gift of yoga with me eight years ago, and I have never left. I return for all the gifts I receive. My life is even more full of love and light due to the practice of yoga."

- Paula R.

"Practicing gentle Kundalini Yoga is the perfect way to experience increased energy and reduced anxiety and stress, to name a few of the benefits of this powerful practice. Gentle classes are accessible to everyone with options presented for all levels of experience and ability. Everybody, yes, everybody, can enjoy and benefit from Yoga."

- Carol B.

Kriyas and Meditations

Kriya for Elevation

This easy set of exercises is excellent as a tune-up. It systematically exercises the spine and aids in the circulation of prana to balance the chakras.

The forward folds, or Life Nerve Stretches, may be modified by only folding forward to tolerance. Rather than aiming for the knees, let the hands slide down the legs and hold where there is a gentle challenge, perhaps knees, shins, or ankles. A yoga strap may also be used in forward folds to provide support. Breath of Fire may be omitted for a very gentle practice, breathing naturally or long and deep instead.

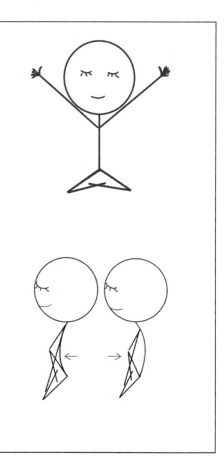

1. Ego Eradicator. Sit in Easy Pose. Raise the arms to a 60 degree angle. Curl the fingertips onto the pads of the palms. Stretch the thumbs so they point upward and inward. Eyes. Closed, concentrate above the head and do Breath of Fire. 1-3 minutes. To end, inhale and touch the thumbs together above the head, and open the fingers. Exhale and apply root lock. Inhale and relax. The exercise opens the lungs, bring the hemispheres of the brain to a state of alertness, and consolidates the magnetic field.

2. Spinal Flex. Sitting in Easy Pose, grasp the shins with both hands. As you inhale, flex the spine forward. As you exhale, flex the spine back, keeping the shoulders relaxed and the head straight. Continue rhythmically with deep breaths for 1-3 minutes. Then inhale, exhale, relax. This exercise stimulates and stretches the lower and middle spine.

3. Spinal Twist. In Easy Pose, grab the shoulders, with the thumbs in back and the fingers in front. Keep the elbows high, with the arms parallel to the ground. Inhale as you twist to the left. Exhale as you twist to the right. Continue 1-4 minutes. To end, inhale facing forward, exhale, and relax.

4. Front Life Nerve Stretch. Stretch both legs straight out in front. Keep your knees straight even if you cannot reach your toes. If you can, grab the toes by wrapping your index and middle finger around the big toes and pressing the big toe nail with your thumbs. In hale the upper body up, keeping the spine straight. Exhale the chest toward the thighs. Bend from the hips and not at the waist. Continue with deep, powerful breathing for 1-3 minutes. Inhale up and hold the breath briefly. Stay up and exhale completely, holding the breath out briefly. Inhale and relax. Exercises 3 and 4 work on the lower and upper spine.

5. Modified Maha Mudra. Sit on the right heel with the left leg extended forward. Beginners can put the right foot against the left inner thigh. Keep the left knee straight even if you can't reach your toes. Grasp the big toes of the left foot with both hands, applying pressure against the toenail. Exhale and bring the elbows toward the ground as you lengthen the core of the spines, bending forward from the navel, continuing the lengthen the spine. Lastly, bring the head toward the knee. Hold, with Breath of Fire for 1-2 minutes. Inhale. Exhale and stretch the head and torso forward and down. Hold the breath out briefly. Inhale, switch legs and repeat the exercise. The exercise helps elimination, stretches the sciatic nerve and brings circulation to the upper torso.

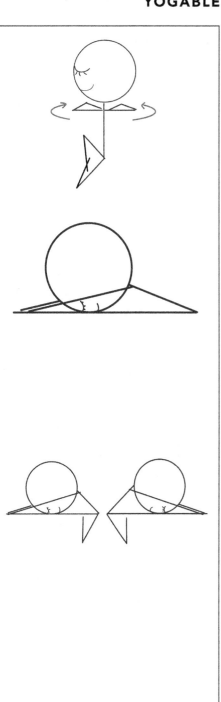

6. Sex Nerve Stretch. Spread the legs wide, keeping the knees straight, grasp the toes as in exercise 4. If you can't reach the toes, keep the hands resting on the legs. Inhale and stretch the spine straight, pulling back on the toes. Exhale and, bending at the waist, bring the head down to the left knee. Inhale up in the center position and exhale down, bringing the head to the right knee. Continue with powerful breathing for 1-2 minutes. Then inhale up in the center position and exhale, bending straight from the waist touching the forehead to the floor. Continue this up and down motion for 1 minute, then inhale up stretching the spine straight. Exhale and bring the forehead to the floor. Hold the breath out briefly as you stretch forward and down. Inhale and relax. This exercise develops flexibility of the lower spine and sacrum and charges the magnetic field.

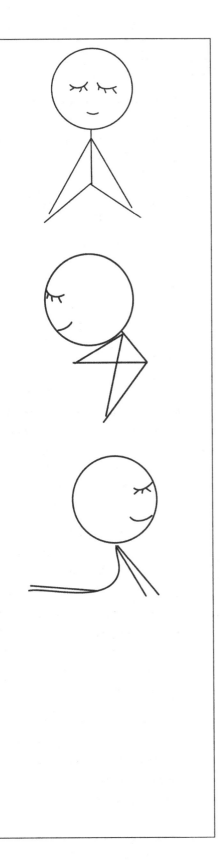

7. Cobra Pose. Lie on the stomach with the palms flat on the floor under the shoulders. The heels are together with the soles of the feet facing up. Inhale into Cobra Pose, arching the spine vertebra by vertebra, front the neck to the base of the spine until the arms are straight. If your hips start to come off the floor, modify the posture to rest on your elbows. Begin Breath of Fire. Continue for 1-3 minutes. Then inhale, arching the spine to the maximum. Exhale and hold the breath out briefly, apply root lock. Inhale. Exhaling slowly, lower the arms and relax the spine from the base of the spine to the top. Relax, lying on the belly with the chin on the floor and arms by the sides. This exercise balances the sexual energy and draws the *prana* to balance *apana* so that the Kundalini energy can circulate to the higher centers in the following exercises. If pressure is felt in the lower back, spread the feet wider apart.

8. Shoulder Shrugs. Sit in Easy Pose. Place the hands on the knees. Inhale and shrug the shoulders up toward the ears. Exhale and drop the shoulders down. Continue rhythmically with powerful breathing for 1-2 minutes. Inhale. Exhale and relax. This exercise balances the upper chakras and opens the higher brain centers.

9. Neck Rolls. Sit in Easy Pose. Begin rolling the neck clockwise in a circular motion, bringing the right ear toward the right shoulder, the back of the head toward the back of the neck, left ear toward the left shoulder and the chin toward the chest. The shoulders remain relaxed and motionless. The neck should be allowed to gently stretch as the head circles around. Continue for 1-2 minutes, then reverse the direction and continue for 1-2 minutes more. Bring the head to a central position and relax.

10. Sat Kriya. Sit on the heels with the arms overhead and the palms together. Interlace the fingers (as pictured) except for the index fingers, which point straight up. Men cross the right thumb over the left: women cross the left thumb over the right. Begin to chant Sat Naam, emphatically in a constant rhythm about 8 times per 10 seconds. Chant the sound Sat from the navel point and solar plexus, and pull the navel all the way in and up. On Naam relax the navel. Continue for 3 minutes, the inhale and pull the root lock. Mentally allow the energy to flow through the top of the skull. Exhale and hold the breath out and pull all the locks. In hale and relax. Sat Kriya circulates the Kundalini energy through the cycle of the chakras, aids in digestions and strengthens the nervous system.

11. Relax on the back with the arms at the sides, palms facing up. Deep relaxation allows you to enjoy and consciously integrate the mind/body changes which have been brought about during the practice of this *kriya*. It allows you to sense the extension of the self through the magnetic field and the aura and allows the physical body to deeply relax.

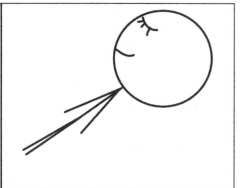

Strengthening the Aura

Your aura is the electromagnetic energy field that surrounds you. When the aura is weak a person feels readily swayed by others, overwhelmed by outside influences, and easily emotional. A strong aura gives you the power of protection (from outside influences and disease,) and projection (clarity of intention). You feel stable and secure in yourself. This allows you to shine and be openhearted.

This is a simple yet powerful *kriya* for keeping disease away, eliminating digestive problems, and developing a strong aura.

Some adjustments are needed to make it user friendly for the whole family, especially the kids. I choose to include this set because of the powerful effects it has on the aura. In addition to the *kriya*, adaptations are given below.

1. Yogic Push-Ups (Down-Dog). Stand up.

   Bend forward and place the palms on the ground shoulder-width apart. The body forms a triangle. Raise the right leg up with the knee straight. The body forms a continuous angle from the buttocks to the extended leg. Exhale, bend the arms and bring the head close to the ground. Inhale, raise the body back to the original position. Continue the push-ups, bending only the elbows for 1 1/2 minutes. Stand up and take a few breaths. Repeat the exercise, raising the left leg, for the same amount of time.

   Down-Dog options from the author:

   a. Remain in traditional Down-Dog.
   b. Raise one leg and hold it off the ground, either high or low, without push-up, hold for 30 seconds, then switch sides.
   c. In Down-Dog with one leg raised add a gentle push-up. The body remains in the shape of a triangle, the elbows bend to allow the head to come down. Practice with each leg extended for 30 seconds.
   d. Begin with 30 second increments and build up the time if desired.

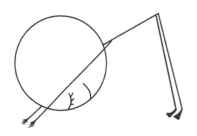

e. Should you be experiencing issues with the wrists, shoulders, ankles, eyes (increased eye pressure or glaucoma), or have vertigo, you can avoid pressure on the joints and the intensity of the inversion by coming into a Half-Dog Pose. This is a Down-Dog with the knees on the ground, in alignment with the hips, with hands and arms stretched straight forward as indicated. Come into Down-Dog and then drop the knees down to the ground.

Postures 2 and 3 can be practiced as described in the set. The author recommends beginning with 30 seconds and building time up as tolerated.

2. Arm Raises. Sit in Easy Pose. Extend the left hand forward as if shaking hands. Bring the right hand underneath the left, and grasp the back of the left hand with the right. Lock the hands together. Both palms facing to the right. Inhale, raise the arms to 60 degree angle above the horizontal. Exhale and return the arms to chest level. Continue this strong chopping motion with a deep and powerful breath for 2-3 minutes keeping the elbows straight. Then inhale, stretching the arms up. Exhale and relax.

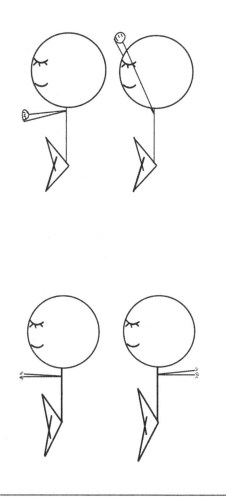

3. Aura Ripples. Extend both arms forward, parallel to the ground with palms facing each other about 6 inches apart. As you inhale, open the arms, stretching them back and toward each other. They drop slightly as they open. Exhale, bring them forward to the original position. Use a deep, rhythmic breath and visualize your arms creating energy ripples that extend your aura further and further. Continue for 2 to 3 minutes.

<u>Kriya for Pelvic Balance</u>

When you move in balance and grace, you feel connected to the earth. This experience is physical as well as mental. When the pelvis and the muscles that shape its posture are out of balance, many systems of the body will begin to show signs of stress. Exhaustion, low endurance, and lower back pain are common symptoms of this condition. This kriya is helpful for staying energetic and balanced, as well as for maintaining potency if practiced regularly.

Approach these exercises slowly and carefully. For a gentle start, begin practicing postures with the shortest recommended time. Adaptations are given by the author. Breath of Fire may be omitted for a very gentle practice.

1. Bridge Pose. Sit with the feet flat on the floor and shoulder-width apart. Place the hands on the floor behind you, fingers pointing away from the body. Raise the body supporting it with straight arms and bent legs. The body from the knees to the shoulders forms a straight line that is parallel to the ground. Let the head fall back slightly. Apply the Root Lock and you hold the posture, breathing normally. Continue for 1-3 minutes. Inhale, exhale, and relax down. This exercise strengthens the back and aids metabolism.

   To modify Bridge Pose, lie on the back, bend the knees so the feet are flat on the floor, close to the buttocks. Head, shoulders, and arms stay on the floor with palms facing down as you lift the hips up while keeping the spine straight. Support the body on feet and shoulders. A very gentle adaptation to this posture may be to lie on the ground with knees bent and feet on the floor, and place a block under the body, length-wise across the lower back, or sacral spine area. Make small adjustments for placement comfort and relax into a supported bridge pose. The block can be used flat on the floor or on its side depending upon personal flexibility of the spine.

2. Wheel Pose. Lie on the back. Bend the legs, with the soles of the feet pressed against the floor, close to the buttocks. Bending the elbows, place the palms of the hands on the floor above the shoulders with the fingers pointing back toward the shoulders. Keeping the feet and knees parallel, begin to carefully lift the body off the floor by pushing against the floor with the hands and feet. Lead with the hips, followed by the chest. The neck arches back as you straighten the elbows. The body forms one continuous arch from the heels to the hands. In this position begin Breath of Fire. Continue for 30 seconds to 3 minutes. Inhale, and exhale to slowly and carefully let yourself down and relax on the back. Wheel Pose strengthens the lower back and muscles of the abdomen and thighs. It facilitates the flow of energy through the spine and aids metabolism.

For a gentle posture, begin as described in gentle Bridge Pose above. For Wheel Pose when lifting the hips arch the spine up, lifting the chest. This is a gentle back bend with the body supported by feet and shoulders. Hands can remain on the floor palms facing down, or fingers can be interlaced and arms drawn under the body. A gentler adaptation to this posture may be to lie on the ground with knees bent and feet on the floor, and place a yoga block flat under the body, length-wise along the spine from the base of the ribs through the upper back. Relax down on the block for a supported, heart-opening back bend. Make small adjustments in block placement for comfort. The head may relax down to the ground, or another block or blanket may be placed under the head if additional support is needed.

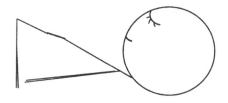

3. Locust Pose with Venus Lock. Lie on your stomach. Bring the chin onto the floor. Clasp the hands in Venus Lock behind the back. Inhale and stretch the arms up straight as you raise the legs as high as possible. Keep the knees and elbows straight as you stretch up. Breath of Fire. Continue for 1-3 minutes. Inhale, exhale, relax. This exercise aids in digestion by circulating energy through the stomach and intestines and tones abdominal muscles.

    Locust may be modified by spreading the feet apart, and reaching arms behind if the hands don't reach to interlace. From here legs can be lifted together, or even one at a time. If hernias or lung issues are present this posture is not safe to practice. Lie on the stomach and rest the forehead on the floor instead. Lying on the stomach is actually good for the colon.

4. Alternate Bends. Stand with your feet straddled. Raise the arms straight overhead with the palms pressed together. Inhale, exhale, twist slightly toward the left, bend, and touch the fingertips to the left foot. Inhale and rise up to the starting position. Exhale, twist slightly toward the right, bend, and touch the fingertips to the right foot.

    Be aware of keeping the arms straight with elbows close to the ears the entire time. Continue rhythmically with powerful breathing for 1-3 minutes. Inhale upright. Exhale and relax. With these movement, the pelvis and the muscle groups on opposite sides of the body are balanced.

    Alternate Bends can be made gentle by bending with the hands down toward the knees on each side instead of the feet.

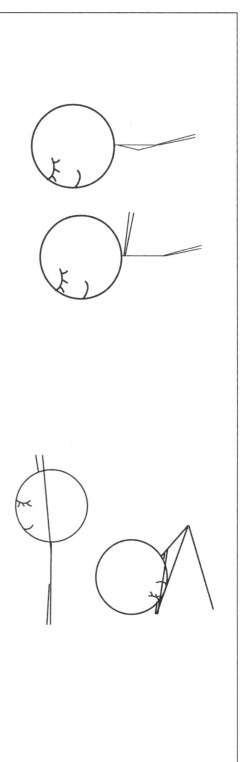

5. Kundalini Lotus. Sit with the soles of the feet together. Wrap the first ginger of each hand around the big toes and press the top of the toes with the thumbs. Lean back slightly and stretch the legs up to a 60-degree angle from the ground. The legs are spread, the knees are straight. Balance on the buttocks. To maintain your balance, keep the eyes open and focus on a point some distance from you. Begin Breath of Fire. Continue 1-3 minutes. Inhale. Exhale and relax. This exercise helps to channel second chakra energy and maintain potency. Pressing the tip of the big toe stimulates the pituitary gland.

This is a balancing posture may begin in Butterfly Pose, placing the soles of the feet together in front of the body. Wrap the index finger and thumb around each big toe and gently begin to lift one or both feet off the ground. Maintain length in the spine without rounding the back. This can be taken deeper by extending one leg out at a 60- degree angle, then switch legs. Come back into Butterfly Pose as needed.

6. Leg Swings. Come into Cow Pose, supporting the body on the hand and knees, both shoulder-width apart. Inhale and stretch the head up and arch the spine. Meanwhile, lift the right leg straight up behind you, keeping the hip straight. Exhale and curve the spine, bringing the knee and forehead together. The spine arches and curves as you continue with the right leg for 1-3 minutes. Inhale and exhale. Then repeat the exercise using the left leg 1-3 minutes. Inhale and exhale. Balances leg and abdominal muscles.

Leg Swings can be practiced with a smaller range of movement, as needed.

7. Relax on the back for 5 minutes or more.

Kirtan Kriya Yoga Meditation

Reproduced from Alzheimer's Research and Prevention Foundation (ARPF) materials by permission. Kirtan Kriya singing exercise is great for anyone interested in improving their brain function and supporting memory. For more information visit www.alzheimersprevention.org.

Kirtan Kriya exercise utilizes the primal sounds – and is meant to be practiced for greater attention, concentration, focus, improved short-term memory, and better mood. The primal sounds consist of:

*   Saa Taa Naa Maa
*   The sounds are chanted repeatedly and in order (i.e., Saa Taa Naa Maa). They come from the mantra 'Sat Nam', which means 'my true essence.'

Kirtan Kriya Instructions

If you would like to practice the Kirtan Kriya singing exercise, here are the basic steps:

1. Repeat the Saa Taa Naa Maa sounds (or mantra) while sitting with your spine straight.
2. If possible, your focus of concentration is the L form, while your eyes are closed.
3. With each syllable, imagine the sound flowing in through the top of your head and out the middle of your forehead (your third eye point).
4. For two minutes, sing in your normal voice.
5. For the next two minutes, sing in a whisper.
6. For the next four minutes, say the sound silently to yourself.
7. Then reverse the order, whispering for two minutes, and then out loud for two minutes, for a total of twelve minutes.
8. To come out of the exercise, inhale very deeply, stretch your hands above your head, and then bring them down slowly in a sweeping motion as your exhale.
9. The finger positions are every important in this kriya.
10. On Saa, touch the index fingers of each hand to your thumbs.
11. On Taa, touch your middle fingers to your thumbs.
12. On Naa, touch your ring fingers to your thumbs.
13. On Maa, touch your little fingers to your thumbs.

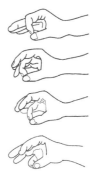

Anti-Hypertension Meditation

Sitting in Easy Pose, place fingertips together forming a teepee, fingers extending out from the heart center. Apply moderate pressure between fingers and thumbs. Keep the eyes 1/10th open and focus at the tip of the nose or at the Third Eye.

Inhale through the mouth to the maximum, and exhale through the nose. Breathe affectionately and beautifully as though you were drinking honey. Listen to the mantra *"Rakhe Rakhanhar,"* and feel the rhythm in your heart, and in every cell of your body. Continue meditation for 11 to 31 minutes. As a modification, begin this meditation with 3 to 5 minutes and build up time to tolerance.

To end, sit quietly and listen to the sound chant back to you. Feel protection and victory.

Comments about the meditation
If you practice this meditation for the full 31 minutes, allow yourself to sleep afterwards.

"At Wits End"
Meditation When You Don't Know What to Do

Sit in Easy Pose or in a chair. Relax the arms down by the sides of the body. Bend the elbows and raise the hands up and in until they meet at the level of the chest. With the palms facing your chest, extend the fingers of each hand. Cross your hands so one palm rests in the other and the thumbs are crossed. The fingers should point up at a comfortable angle. It does not matter whether your left or right hand is on top. With your eyes closed, focus on the center point just above the eyebrows. Then bring your focus to the tip of your nose. Follow this four-step breathing sequence:

- Inhale through the nose, then exhale through the nose.
- Inhale through the mouth, then exhale through the mouth.
- Inhale though the nose, then exhale through the mouth.
- Inhale through the mouth, then exhale through the nose.

All breaths should be deep, complete, and powerful. When breathing through the mouth, purse the lips almost as if to whistle. Continue this sequence for 11-31 minutes. Sit in this place of stillness.

Beginners may start with 3 minutes of meditation.

7

Very Gentle Yoga; Can We Be Kinder?

"Compassion for others begins with kindness to ourselves."

- Pema Chodron (2008)

Can we be kinder? The answer is *yes*! Show up and say *yes*! Another reminder here: these are guidelines based on experience. Be creative and find your personal path. Your mat, sheepskin, or chair is your own personal laboratory for research.

Why Very Gentle Yoga?

Years into teaching a basically gentle yoga practice, I realized there was a need for more kindness to the physical body. A need to take it down another notch for Very Gentle Yoga. This type of yoga is good for those who are chronically ill or recovering from illness, memory-impaired, motion-limited, or anyone who wants a slow and gentle stretch for the body, as well as stimulation for the mind. Moving the body helps support healthy mental function. Physical exercise allows us to access higher realms of consciousness than the mind can access on its own.

I frequently remind students of all levels that it's our job to listen to and honor what the body needs on a daily basis. What the body needs today may be different from what it needed yesterday or will need tomorrow. It's okay to challenge the body and the mind in yoga, as well as in life, but we never use force – challenge, but don't force!

We don't force, we serve. It is in the spirit of service that I override the common "no shoes in the yoga studio" policy for very gentle or special needs yoga classes. In addition to wheelchairs, leg braces, and medical boots, I welcome shoes inside the yoga room for those who need them to walk comfortably. The yoga studio is honored as a sacred space and typically it is entered with the feet bare. Delivering yoga and serving students is an honor that, in my opinion, takes precedence over the typical "no shoes" rule. While I allow exceptions to the typical rule in my own studio, if you are a yoga teacher, you'll have to decide what works for your space. Disposable shoe covers are an affordable option. For a personal practice at home this probably won't be an issue.

This talk of feet and shoes reminds me of a story I am very fond of about the teachings of Guru Nanak. Enjoy the below excerpt from a passage titled *Mecca – The Kaaba* from the book *Guru for the Aquarian Age – The Life and Teachings of Guru Nanak* (1996).

The keeper of the Kaaba – a sacred building in Mecca – one night discovered that the Guru was sleeping with his feet towards the Kaaba. It was time for prayer so he informed the priest that a pilgrim was committing a great sacrilege by turning his feet towards the house of God. The incensed priest rushed to where the Guru was sleeping.

"Wake up, you stupid fool," he screamed, "and rub your face on the ground and beg to be forgiven for turning your feet towards the house of God."

The Guru did not move, but quietly said, "Turn my feet towards the place where God does not dwell."

The priest could no longer control himself and ordered the keeper to take Nanak by the feet and turn him around in the other direction. The door keeper obeyed but whichever direction they turned his feet the Kaaba turned with them. The priest stood spell-bound. He saw that the house of God was in all directions.

The Guru rose and looked at the priest with eyes full of compassion. "Your eyes have been opened for just a moment," he said. "Don't forget what you have seen. All space is nothing but God's dwelling place."

All are welcome in the pursuit and practice of yoga. After all, yoga is union.

What are students looking for in a Very Gentle Yoga class?

Students are looking for a practice that allows for movement and exercise with variations to accommodate how well their bodies are functioning on any given day. Very gentle yoga students want to keep their bodies moving and flexible at their own level of fitness, just enough to challenge them without causing strain or injury. I find that those seeking a very gentle yoga class may also be concerned with brain health and strengthening their powers of memory. Many of these students are elderly and, having heard that yoga and meditation may be good for their memory, they come seeking support for the mind as well as for the body.

Things I avoid in Very Gentle Yoga:
- Breath of Fire. Although I find Breath of Fire compatible for gentle yoga, when we're taking it down a notch for very gentle yoga, I suggest eliminating the powerful breath and rather focusing on a proper natural breath and/or long deep breathing.
- Down Dog
- Frogs and Crows. Instead, we perform ¼ squats or what I refer to as "dips."
- Jumping. Marching or walking in place is a great substitute.
- Too much sitting on the floor; seated poses may often be modified into standing, or even lying down. (This will not apply if practicing yoga in a chair.)
- Multiple exercises performed while stabilizing on the hands and knees

What I add to Very Gentle Yoga:

Blankets, cushions, possible props, permission to visualize, and a can-do attitude!

The same warm-ups given in the chapter "Cushions, Chairs and Choices" may be used in very gentle yoga too. Times can be shorter and the pace can be slower if needed. Again, very gentle yoga allows us to be easier with the body, but it doesn't necessarily mean the practice itself is easy. We do work the body and mind with this practice.

Let's try a great little variation of Spinal Flex now. This is an adapted and supported version of Spinal Flex that I learned from a favorite Hatha yoga teacher of mine. Lie on the ground with your knees bent and both feet flat on the floor. Slowly raise your lower back up in a gentle Spinal Flex, inhaling as the lower back comes up slightly off the floor, then exhaling as you release and round the lower back down against the floor. This Spinal Flex variation is done slowly, is powerful in its subtlety, and amazing for the lower back.

Utilize cushions and blankets and other props to support the body as outlined for the practice throughout this book to provide maximum comfort.

When teaching public yoga classes, I find that the population seeking a very gentle experience may need visual demonstration and visual support throughout the class. As I observe students to make sure they are practicing in a safe way, I have found it is helpful if I continue with the yoga postures myself, do more of the yoga with them to help them keep on track and keep up. Typically, the teacher gives instruction and demonstration of posture and then the class practices the exercise for the specified amount of time while the teacher monitors. I noticed early on in teaching seniors that I if I simply demonstrate and stop to monitor, many of them end the posture as well. A contributing factor in this is loss of hearing as we age. I find students with hearing loss are closely watching visual cues and follow along by copying the teacher.

Potential students may or may not be aware that there is hearing impairment, and therefore may not verbalize their needs for volume. In a class setting it is important to project your voice throughout the room. This is true in any class, but a little more volume may be needed when you have persons with hearing loss in attendance. Shouting is not an appropriate alternative, so occasionally you may need to make a recommendation for private sessions for those who simply cannot hear well enough in a group setting to follow along in a safe manner.

I also recommend revisiting the breath frequently. Many times, students are unaware that they are holding their breath. Give frequent reminders to check in with the breath in order to keep it flowing. I find it can be typical for students new to yoga to breathe in a paradoxical way, where the belly contracts on the inhale and expands on the exhale. Make sure that the breath and body are moving in proper conjunction, the belly should expand on the inhale and contract on the exhale. Work first to find the natural breath and then later to coordinate long deep breathing. Keep it simple!

Although in my background with Kundalini yoga we traditionally practice without props, the idea being that the body is in the posture where it is supposed to be, I find that props, verbal reminders, and posture demonstration can be beneficial and supportive while helping to prevent injury. Listen, listen, and listen some more, and remember that what is needed can change daily.

Recommended Yoga Sets and Kriya: (Found at the end of the chapter.)
Warm-Up Exercise Set
Kriya for Elevation, as found in the previous chapter.
Exercises for Maintaining a Flexible Spine
Pregnancy yoga sets are a hidden treasure for a very gentle approach to yoga. Wonderful sets are available by those who specialize in pregnancy yoga.

Please follow directions for deep relaxation in the previous chapter upon completion of the yoga *kriya*. Meditation will typically follow the period of deep relaxation. The *kriyas* in this chapter are given as originally taught, followed by additional comments from the author for gentle modifications.

Recommended Meditations: (Found at the end of the chapter.)
Kirtan Kriya, as found in the previous chapter
Safeguard Your Heart, or Cross Heart *Kirtan Kriya* Meditation
Meditation for a Calm Heart

Several meditations in this book include the mantra *Sa Ta Na Ma* while conjointly using pressure on the fingertips. Two of the meditations listed above each work the finger tips, which stimulate nerve endings connecting to the brain. As we age it is important to do activities that put pressure on the finger tips to maintain a healthy brain.

The word mantra comes from *Man-* mind and *Trang-* wave or projection. Mantra is described as a science, as it is based on sound and energy having a predictable effect on the human being. Mantra vibrates through the mind and body, creating a special heat that leads to clearing and neutrality. This book offers soundtrack links for accompanying music proper pronunciation of mantras. The links can be found at the end of the book with listed mantras.

"Mantras are a powerful healing force, because of the vibratory effects of their sounds. If a tree falls in the forest and no one is there to hear it, does it make a sound? Of course not. It only makes a vibration. Sound only occurs when vibrations strike the eardrum and are carried to the brain. This is just a way of pointing out the fact that every sound also has a vibration. Particular vibrations can strongly stimulate the glands of the endocrine system, especially those located in the head and neck. This includes the pituitary, the system's master gland, as well as the hypothalamus.

Different mantras have markedly different effects upon the function of the endocrine system. In one interesting experiment at the University of Arizona, my colleague Gurucharan Singh Khalsa, Ph.D., observed brain function with a PET scan and noted that during the chanting of the mantra "Sa Ta

Na Ma,' there was a strong shift in brain activity to the right frontal and parietal regions. This shift indicated an improvement in mood and alertness.

It has been shown that chanting certain yoga mantras stimulates the vagus nerve, the most important single nerve in the body. The vagus nerve, which travels through the neck near the jaw, services the heart, lungs, intestinal tract, and back muscles.

Sound currents also strongly influence the nadis and chakras by vibrating the upper palate of the mouth, which has eighty-four points connected to the body's ethereal energy system. Some of the points carry energy directly to the hypothalamus and to the pituitary. Striking these points on the plate with the tongue has been compared to striking the key of a computer with your finger – the act of striking is simple, but the effect can be profound." [2]

Reproduced from *Meditation as Medicine* by Dharma Singh Khalsa, MD (2001, Simon and Schuster) by permission of the author. Copyright 2001, Simon and Schuster. For more information on Dr. Dharma Khalsa's work, visit www.drdharma.com

Reported Benefits and Testimonials:
- Improved body-mind connection
- Improved sense of well-being
- Continued learning
- Feelings better about self and others
- Feeling better mentally and physically
- The ability to go at your own pace
- The "*flexibility to tie my own shoes*"
- Feeling of increased spiritual connection
- Decreased pain with regular gentle movement of the body

"I have been practicing gentle Kundalini Yoga for sixteen years. When I began, I was physically ill, barely able to walk, and had pains throughout my body. Today I am active and pain-free, which I mainly attribute to my gentle yoga practice."

- Dr. Michael R.

"I have leukemia and I find that the breathing exercises and the stretching and strengthening of muscles are a clear benefit for the condition of my health. The atmosphere of gentle yoga is friendly, comforting, and not competitive in any way. I feel stronger and supported."

- Ann P.

---

[2] The Gurucharan Singh Khalsa Ph.D. referred to in the University of Arizona study is not the same Gurucharan Singh Khalsa quoted elsewhere in this book. Both, however, are doctors of psychology and are respected members of the Kundalini yoga community.

"To me, gentle yoga is comforting yoga. The more comfortable I feel, the better I will respond to the yoga process. I attended my first yoga class with great hesitation. Would I be able to do yoga? Would I be able to keep up? Would I feel out of place? From the moment class started, all my fears left. Not only was I able to follow along; if I showed any hesitation, I was quickly given an adapted version of posture, or reminded that I could just continue to breathe in a comfortable place. I have been forever grateful that this was my first experience with yoga."

-Jennifer S.

Kriyas and Meditations

Warm-Up Exercise Set

This is a fabulous set for warming up and stretching the body. This is not an actual *kriya*, but a complete warm-up set taught in 1974. To begin exercise times can be shortened to 1 minute each, slowly building to 2 to 3 minutes if desired. Take care of knees with alternate seated postures if needed, such as Easy Pose or sitting in a chair.

The series of forward folds, or Life Nerve Stretches, exercises 6 and 7 may be modified by only folding forward to tolerance. Rather than aiming for the knees, let the hands slide down the legs and hold where there is a gentle challenge, perhaps knees, shins, or ankles. A yoga strap may also be used in forward folds to provide support.

1. Spinal Flex. Sitting on the heels, flex the spine back and forth, inhaling as it arches forward, exhaling as the spine contracts back. Continue for 2-3 minutes.	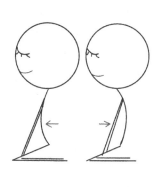

2. Spinal Twist. Sitting on the heels, with hands on the shoulders, fingers in front, thumbs in back, twist spine side to side for 2-3 minutes.

3. Shoulder Shrugs. Relax hands down on Knees, and inhale raising shoulders up to ears, exhale relaxing them down. Repeat for 2-3 minutes.

4. Neck Rolls. Tilt the chin down to the chest and gently circle the head, breathing slowly and deeply, keeping the shoulders relaxed. Make slow, smooth circles, ironing out any kinks as you go. Continue for 1-2 minutes, reverse for another 1-2 minutes.

5. Cat Cow Pose. Come onto the hands and knees. The hands are shoulder-width apart with the fingers facing forward. The knees are directly below the hips. Inhale and tilt the pelvis forward, arching the spine down, and stretching the head and neck back. Then exhale and tilt the pelvis the opposite way, arching the spine up and bring the chin to the chest. Continue for 2-3 minutes.

6. Life Nerve Stretches:
   a. Both legs stretched out in front, bend at the hips and grab toes. Exhale as you fold forward and the head comes down toward the knees, rise up as you inhale, head following. Continue moving up and down for 1-2 minutes.
   b. Legs stretched out in front, bend the left knee and place the left heel in the right thigh, and repeat inhaling up and exhaling down over the leg for 1-2 minutes. Switch legs and repeat for 1-2 minutes.

7. Wide Leg Forward Fold. Stretch legs out in front and then stretch them out wide. Fold forward and hold on to the toes. Inhale up, and exhale down to alternate knees. Continue for 1-2 minutes.

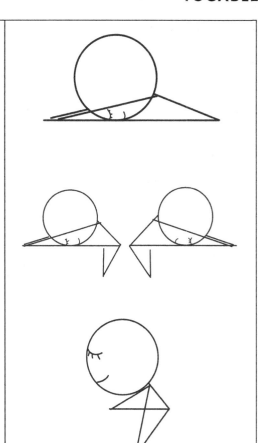

PATTY (PATWANT) WILDASINN

<u>Kriya for Elevation</u>

This set can be found in its entirety in Chapter 6. For a very gentle practice, omit Breath of Fire, and begin all exercises at 1 minute. For any issues with the shoulders, the *Sat Kriya mudra* may be held at the heart center rather than over the head in exercise 10.

<u>Exercises for Maintaining a Flexible Spine</u>

Low back pain is one of the most common health complaints of adults one of the most common causes of absenteeism. A quick fix for a back ache is not as easy as a quick energy pick up. The best way to avoid back aches is to do preventative exercises.

This series of exercises works systematically from the base of the spine to the top. All 26 vertebrae receive stimulation and all the energy centers receive a burst of energy. There is increased circulation to the spinal fluid which contributes to greater mental clarity. This series will give increased vitality, help prevent backaches, reduce tension, and keep you young by increasing the flexibility of the spine.

This can be done in the morning as a way to give you added energy for the day. It can also be done in the evening before dinner to revitalize you after a busy day and give you energy for the evenings.

To begin a gentle practice, exercise times can be shortened to 1 minute each, slowly building to 2 to 3 minutes if desired. Take care of knees with alternate seated postures if needed, such as Easy Pose or sitting in a chair. Omit Breath of Fire for a very gentle practice.

1. Rotate the Pelvis. Sit in Easy Pose. Place the hands on the knees. Deeply roll the pelvis around in a grinding motion. Do 26 rotations in each direction. This exercise starts opening up the energy in the lower spine and aids in digestion.

2. Spinal Flex. Sit in Easy Pose, grab the ankles. As you inhale, flex the spine forward, keeping the shoulders relaxed and the head straight. Do not move the head up and down. Exhale and relax the spine back. Continue rhythmically with deep breaths for 1-3 minutes or up to 108 times. As you inhale feel the energy go down the spine and as you exhale feel it come back up to the third eye. Bring *Sat* down and *Nam* back up the spine. To end, inhale deep, hold it, apply root lock, exhale and relax. Feel the energy circulate. This exercise stimulates and stretches the lower spine.

3. Spinal Flex on Heels. Sit on the heels (Rock Pose,) place the hands flat on the thighs. Continue Spinal Flex as above. This exercise works higher up the spine.

4. Neck Rolls. Roll the neck slowly in one direction and then in the other. Continue for at least one minute in each direction. Do this very methodically so that you to not skip, but work out areas of tension. This exercise removes tension in the neck and stimulates the thyroids.

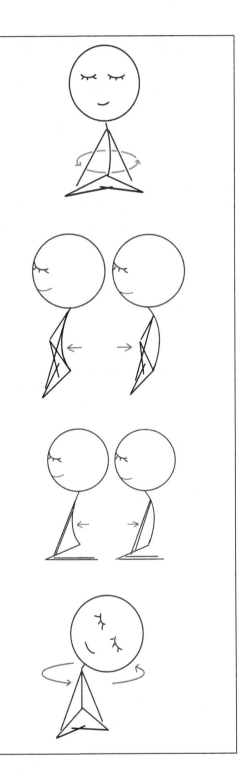

5. Shoulder Stand & Plow Pose. On the back, raise the legs and torso above the head, supporting the body with the hands at the waist and extending the legs and hips into a straight line, with long, deep breathing for 1-2 minutes. Then drop the feet back over the head into Plow Pose, resting arms on the ground. Rest there a minute before slowly lowering hips onto floor, vertebra by vertebra. This exercise bends and stretches the entire spine, especially the neck and thoracic vertebrae. It stimulates the thyroid and the throat chakra, and relaxes and energizes the spine.

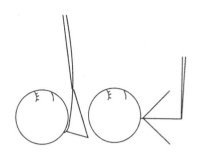

For a gentle Shoulder Stand, lie on the back with the hands palms down next to the hips, or tucked under the hips for increased support, as you raise the legs up in a straight line. The knees may be bent slightly if tension is felt in the lower back. To move into an adapted Plow Pose, bring the knees into the chest and wrap the arms around the legs as you stretch the lower back.

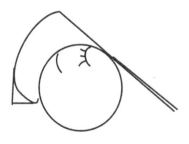

6. Fish Pose. Sit in Lotus Pose, or with legs outstretched, and lie back on the elbows, arching the sternum up, with the weight on the top of the head and the hips. Grab big toes with opposite fingers and do Breath of Fire or long, deep breathing for 1-2 minutes. (With legs stretched out in front, rest on hips, elbows under the shoulders.) Fish Pose is the counter-pose for Plow and Shoulder Stand. It prevents or corrects rounded shoulders and jutting neck. It also stimulates the thyroid and the throat chakra.

Fish Pose is a deep stretch, so take care when practicing. The neck may be kept tucked in toward the neck with a Neck Lock to protect the cervical spine, or dropped back gently instead of coming back to rest on the ground. The gentle option is pictured.

7. Side Twists. Sit on the heels (Rock Pose) or in Easy Pose (as shown), place the hands on the shoulders, fingers in front and thumbs in back. Inhale, twist to the left, exhale twist to the right. Twist your head to each side as well. Gradually feel an increased rotation in your spine. Keep elbows parallel to the ground. To end, inhale to center, hold the breath, apply root lock, exhale, relax and feel the energy circulate. Continue 1-2 minutes or 26 times. This exercise can be done standing up, allowing the arms to swing freely with the body. This exercise opens up the heart center and stimulated the upper spine.

8. Side Bends. In Easy Pose, clasp hands behind neck in Venus Lock and bend straight sideways at the waist to touch elbow on the floor beside the hip, and then reverse. Inhale as you bend left, exhale as you bend right. Don't' arch or contract the back but bend sideways only. Do 1-2 minutes or 26 times. This exercise can be done standing (as pictured), allowing the arms to swing freely. Side Bends are good for the liver and colon and for spinal flexibility.

9. Shoulder Shrugs. Sit on the heels or in Easy Pose, shrug both shoulders up with the inhale and won with the exhale. Inhale up, hold, apply Root Lock, relax. Do for less than 2 minutes. This exercise loosens up the tension in the shoulders.

10. Cobra Pose. Lie on the floor with the palms on the floor under the shoulders. As you inhale, slowly arch the spine up, leading with the nose, then chin, then pushing off with your hands, vertebra by vertebra, until you are arched back as far as possible with no strain in the lower back, concentrating on a good stretch from the heart center up. Breathe long and deep or do Breath of Fire. To end, inhale, hold, pull the energy up the spine and exhale, very slowly, one vertebra at a time come down. Relax 1-3 minutes. This exercise strengthens the lower back, removes tension in the back and balances the flow of sexual energy with navel energy.

For a gentle cobra keep the elbows on the floor under the shoulders with the forearms and palms on the ground in front of you, like a Sphinx, and arch up from this position.

11. Rock and Roll on Spine. Bring your knees to your chest, grab them with the arms, and rock back and forth on the spine, massaging it gently from the neck to the base of the spine for 1-2 minutes. This exercise circulates energy and relaxes the spine.

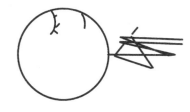

Gentle alternatives include a small rock up and down along the sacral spine, or rocking side to side.

12. Alternate Leg Stretches. Spread the legs wide apart, grasping the toes or any other place on the legs where it is possible to keep the knees straight. Inhale center and exhale down to the left leg, inhale center, and exhale down to the right leg. Continue with powerful breathing.

Inhale center, hold the breath, apply Root Lock and then relax. Bring the legs together and bounce them up and down a few times to relax the muscles and massage them. Loosen up the muscles, but do not strain them. Bend from the lower back and get a good stretch 1-2 minutes.

13. Life Nerve Stretch. Legs outstretched, bring right foot into left thigh, and slowly bend over the left leg to grab the foot or ankle (or whatever is comfortable), keeping the leg flat on the ground. Breathe long and deep or do Breath of Fire for 1-2 minutes. Inhale deeply and slowly come up. Bounce legs and massage them. Switch sides and repeat. This exercise stretches leg muscles and lower back.

14. Cat-Cow. Come on the knees and the hands, inhale as you flex our spine down and bring your head up. Exhale as you flex your spine up in an arched position with the head down to the neck. Keep the arms straight. Continue rhythmically with powerful breathing, gradually increasing the speed as your spine become more and more flexible. Inhale in saggy cow, hold, pull the energy up the spine, exhale and relax on the heels. Sit and slow down the breath and feel the energy circulate. Concentrate at the third eye. 1-3 minutes. This exercise is known as the self-chiropractor. Done regularly, it loosens up and adjusts the spine.

15. Pick Me Up Exercise. Lie down on your back and just relax for a moment. Then bend your knees and draw the heels up towards the buttocks, keeping the feet flat on the floor.

Grab your ankles and holding on the them, slowly raise the hips up, arching the lower spine and lifting the navel towards the sky. As you lift up, slowly inhale the breath through your nose. Hold the breath as you gently stretch up. Lifting as high as is comfortable., then slowly relax down again as you breathe out through the nose. Slowly repeat this lifting up and down movement a minimum of twelve times, synchronizing the breathing with the movement of the hips, and a maximum of 26 lifts. To go from 12 to 26, increase your total by 1-2 lifts per day. To end, inhale up, hold the breath for ten seconds, then relax down, stretching the legs out. Relax and feel the energizing effect of the exercise. This exercise release abdominal stress! It gives you an immediate boost of energy throughout your body that lasts well into the day. It also stimulates your thyroid and allows you to breath deeper. Keep the hands down by the hips as a gentle option.

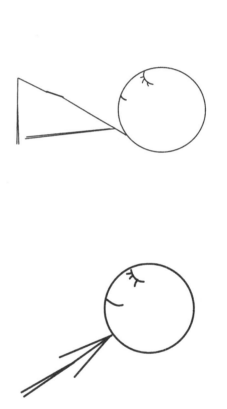

16. Relaxation. Deeply relax on your back, hands to the side, palms facing up.

Exercise tips: People with any history of lower back pain should check with their doctor before beginning. Try to let your breathing do the work, and keep the eyes closed throughout the exercises so that you can feel your body move without visual distractions.

<u>Kirtan Kriya Meditation</u>

This meditation is outlined completely in the previous chapter. For a very gentle practice this meditation may easily be done while seated in a chair.

Chant the mantra *Saa Taa Naa Maa* while pressing the corresponding fingers together. This primal sound translates into the cycle of life; Infinity, Life, Death and Rebirth.

2 minutes aloud.
2 minutes whisper.
3 minutes silent.
2 minutes whisper.
2 minutes aloud.

Sit quietly for one minute. Then inhale, stretch the arms overhead and shake them. Relax.

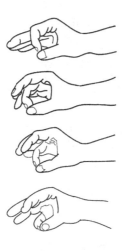

"Safeguard Your Heart" or Cross-Heart Kirtan Kriya

Sit in Easy Pose or in a chair. Cross the forearms, below the wrists, and hold them in front of the chest. Arms out slightly, palms up and facing toward the chest. Look down the tip of the nose.

Begin to chant "Sa Ta Na Ma", one cycle per breath. With each syllable, touch the thumb tip to the fingertip of the index finger with "Sa," then thumb to middle finger with "Ta," thumb to ring finger with "Na," and thumb to little finger on "Ma." Continue for 11-31 minutes. To finish, inhale; hold your breath and roll your eyes up; become completely still. Exhale and relax in stillness.

PATTY (PATWANT) WILDASINN

<u>Meditation for a Calm Heart</u>

Sit in Easy Pose or in a chair, with a light neck lock. Either close the eyes or look straight head with the eyes half open.

Place the left hand on the center of the chest at the heart-center level. The palm is flat against the chest and the fingers are parallel to the ground, pointing to the right. The right hand is raised up to the right side of the body as if taking an oath. The palm is facing forward, and the first finger is curled into the thumb in active Gyan Mudra. The rest of the fingers are straight. The forearm is perpendicular to the ground. Concentrate on the flow of the breath. Feel it consciously. Inhale slowly and deeply through the nose. Suspend the breath as it is locked in. Retain the breath as long as possible. Then exhale smoothly, gradually and completely. When the breath is totally exhaled, suspend the breath out for as long as possible. Continue this pattern for a specified amount of time, then inhale, exhale strongly 3 times, and relax.

<u>Comments about the meditation</u>
This meditation is perfect for beginners. It opens your awareness of the breath and conditions the lungs. It is recommended for beginners to start with 3 minutes, and gradually work up to 11. The maximum time it can be performed is 31 minutes.

The entire posture induces a feeling of calmness. On an emotional level, it clarifies your perception in relationship to yourself and others. It creates a still point for the prana at the heart center.

Additionally, when you hold the breath in or out for "as long as possible" you should not gasp or be under strain when you let the breath move again.

8

Special Needs Family Yoga

"Whenever I look at another and fail to see God, I know that I must look again."
- The Poetry of Michael (2018)

*"When spiritual teachers talk of mankind being "one," the oneness to which they refer
is our one desire to be happy and free. We all share that same desire and the same fear.
If more of us began to choose love, then oneness would be restored. It starts with you.
You have a major part in the healing of the world. The more oneness you create in
your life, the more light you shine on everyone around you. I believe this is our biggest
mission here on earth. To choose love to restore oneness, and shine our light."*
- Gabrielle Bernstein, *"The Universe Has Your Back"* (2016)

Much of this chapter is directed to yoga teachers and those who wish to bring a special needs yoga class to their space or community. Some of the guidelines for setting up a class will not apply to a personal practice in the home. However, the yoga themed classes are designed for all kids and families, regardless of ability. Take what you can use!

As I sit down to write this chapter, I know what I want to say. I've had a written outline for months, and it's been in my head for years. And yet, all I can do is take a deep sigh and think, *"So, you want to teach yoga to special needs kids and adults? Bless you!"* This population will love you and challenge you. They are honest, and they can be loud or very subdued. You may be touched, smelled, licked, and hugged, or just as easily ignored and dismissed. One minute your heart may be so full you're simply bursting with love, and the next you are asking yourself, *"Why am I doing this?"*

Before saying yes, be aware these kids will be your teachers. They will stretch you to grow, maybe beyond your comfort zone. They will push you to be a better person, and they will hold you accountable. It's really not for the faint of heart. Now, let's continue.

How do we begin a special needs yoga class? Start by saying "Yes, you are welcome here. The whole family is welcome here." I am very big on family style yoga for the special needs population. As the parent of a special needs child, I have spent many hours in waiting rooms and on the sidelines, with other worn-out parents, while my child participates in therapies, treatments, and sports. When I started teaching Special Needs Family Yoga, it was with the intention to include parents, to provide an activity where the special needs child, siblings, and parents may participate together. It's all inclusive! Family yoga class is geared toward helping kids (adult children too) and their parents, where everyone benefits.

We work on balance, strength, flexibility, focus, and concentration, but the kids and special needs students just think we're having fun. Yogic techniques are also taught to stimulate the brain, release stress and anxiety, and encourage deep relaxation. The parents need deep relaxation as much, if not more, than the kids!

Another reason I strongly advocate family participation in special needs yoga is that each child has unique differences and abilities, be they physical or behavioral, and the parent or caregiver is best equipped to deal with their child. I present a class, demonstrate, and redirect, but ultimately let the accompanying adult maintain control of any physical or behavior management. For instance, the parent or caregiver of a child with Cerebral Palsy will be able to support their child in yoga without pushing stiff muscles beyond what is right for the individual. Similarly, a tantrum or outburst may be best managed by the parent or caregiver who knows the child, rather than the yoga teacher. I feel family participation best serves the safety of the community during a yoga class. When teaching in a school setting it is important to have the teacher and/or teacher aides present for support.

There are definitely times when the student will better respond to requests and motivation from the teacher over the parent. If you are teaching you are holding the space, so by all means give direction, the caregiver is there for backup and for their own yoga experience.

Many years ago, I had an Ayurvedic doctor tell me that in India it is seen as a blessing for a family to receive a special needs child because it means they are finishing their karma. I'll take it! The road is hard for many families, and yoga can deliver a flip of the switch – a shift from exhaustion and frustration to gratitude and wonder, even if it's just for an hour.

Several years back, I wrote this real-life story describing a day in the life of a parent with a special needs child. This story could apply to all parents. The point of sharing is to demonstrate that we never know what people are walking through on any given day, so it's important to receive others with a neutral mind and an open heart.

A Day in My Life
January 21, 2016

I opened my daily meditation book this morning and read, "When we hoard what we have been given, we block the door to receiving more." All I could do was laugh! I was having a morning alright, tired of being on duty 24/7. I'd love to share what I'd been given this morning, but doubt there would be any takers. I had just finished cleaning up a "bathroom blowout." I'll spare the details and just say when we were planning for kids some twenty years ago, I didn't think that as the baby reached eighteen, I'd still be cleaning up toileting messes. I feel worn out, and this morning I don't want to brush anyone's teeth other than my own. Hell, I've been scheduling babysitters for twenty years! I'd like to say the "bathroom blowout" is rare, but I'd be lying. Who wants some of this? I don't want to hoard.

Later in the day, I reflect on a trip to the store, where I overheard a woman talking poorly about a special needs child and his mother, neither of whom were present.

Evidently, she was bothered that the mother lets the child play with toys that are too young for his actual age, but ultimately decided it was "okay" because, "he's not really all there anyway." Me - disbelief! Let me tell you that those of us who have children with special needs, KNOW them to be COMPLETE and WHOLE just the way they are. We love them as much as we love our typical children, as much as you love your children. Parenting is hard, period! If you get the urge to talk bad about someone else, please remember you don't know what kind of "bathroom blowout" they may be walking through every day.

Mothers of special needs kids are some of the strongest women I have ever met. These kids push their families - moms, dads, and siblings - to grow in ways we would never have dreamed of or chosen on our own. These kids and families inspire me, and renew my energy for life! So yeah, I'd be more than happy to share some of what's been given to me. Along with a poopy bathroom, I've been given patience, compassion, strength, and undying love. Blessings to all!"

Defining class parameters:

I'd like to reiterate that the classes outlined in this book are good for neuro-typical children or universal family style yoga classes, as well as those of all ages with special needs. I use the terms "typical," "normal," and "special needs" as description words only, not as labels, with respect to the fact that we are all different. Only slightly greater than 20% of the population has to display the same pattern in physical make-up or behavior to be considered "normal." The practice outlined is good for all of our vast human differences and similarities.

If you picked up this book to provide a practice for you and your child in the privacy of your own home, some of the class information will not apply. Just know the technology of yoga can be as healing for you as it is beneficial for your child. Most importantly, get into your creative flow and have fun!

I am fully aware there are places and events in life where it is not appropriate to bring our special needs children and place on them unreasonable behavior goals. As a parent out and about with my young, unpredictable Autistic son, I have been the recipient of dread, nastiness, and pity. These add to an already exhausting load. It's a bummer to be the mom with the kid nobody wants to see coming! I share this to emphasize that my overall goal with special needs yoga is to create a space where all who attend are welcome and accepted. I once had a mother come to me, a month or so into participating in yoga classes, practically in tears while thanking me for not asking them to leave. She had just been waiting to be asked to leave due to her son's noises and sporadic movement. To create a safe and welcoming space, basic parameters must be set.

Who is welcome?

In creating a public or private class it is up to you, as the teacher, to decide what population/ populations you may wish to serve. I personally welcome anyone and everyone in special needs classes. I typically have students on the Autism Spectrum, those with Down Syndrome, ADHD, Tourette's Syndrome, pervasive developmental delays, and sensory processing issues. I have also had a student who was non-verbal, blind and in a wheelchair participate in yoga. That's *Yogable!*

What ages may participate?

In a private yoga studio setting, I welcome all ages. When promoting a class through a city or recreation department, I typically set the age from seven to adult, and then possibly teach a separate class for younger children. If you are teaching in a school setting, gear each class toward the targeted age group.

Is there any behavior that will exclude participation?

Occasionally students may come in who are overly disruptive. (Disruptive is kind of the norm with this population, so I add the "overly" to indicate the extreme.) It has been my experience that this takes care of itself as participation continues. However, violent and explosive behavior is not appropriate in a group class setting and a referral or private class may need to be offered.

What about parent participation?

While it is beneficial for parents to stay in class to assist their kids as needed as well as to direct their behavior, I ultimately want them to stay for the experience. The parents of special needs kids are some of the strongest people I know, but their nervous systems have been depleted and stretched to the limit. I encourage independent parent participation in class as much as possible. Sometimes the parents need permission not to hover and micro-manage. Some families find each person is able to participate independently with only minor redirection from the parent. In other families, parents find they need to shadow and help their children participate throughout the class. There is no right or wrong, simply what works for each family.

The mothers of special needs children are often more emotionally contracted and exhausted than their children. It's not intentional. They desperately need a system of support. Their senses may be heightened in fight mode, or dulled in flight mode, always on alert or simply shut down. It is ideal when these parents are able to transition into a practice just for their own self-care, in addition to the special needs family class.

Should students sit in rows or in a circle?

Participants may be set up in rows facing the teacher, or in a large circle. Setting students up in a large circle offers more visual connection and interaction with peers. Sitting in rows offers less visual stimulation and distraction. There are pros and cons to both, so experiment: take your set-up cue from what best serves the student needs. I do suggest seating students with more than arms-length distance between them so they can't easily reach over and touch their neighbor. I do not encourage activities that involve touching beyond the parent child pair. This may sound counterintuitive to those who are already actively teaching kids yoga, but trust me. I do invite student to pass tings to each other for sharing activities, but otherwise creating an environment that supports keeping the hand to the self is wise for students with poor impulse control and those with weak or overly strong personal boundaries.

What's a good time to hold class?

Obviously, you want to choose a time when most kids and adults will be available to attend. Early evenings and weekends are best. Class duration is best kept to forty-five minutes or less. An hour may be too long to hold the attention of young children and students of all ages with special needs. An important thing to consider is choosing a time when you will have the space to yourself. I recommend that studio space not be shared during special needs yoga so as not to disturb other classes, or healing modalities. As hard as you may try, you can let go of formal studio and social etiquette. By all means, teach appropriate studio/social behavior, just don't be attached to the outcome.

With parameters set and preparations made, remind yourself to show up with an open mind and without expectation. Present the class, but don't worry about making the kids do the postures, or waiting on all of them to do the postures. There may be students who only partially participate as well as those you may feel aren't doing much, but they still benefit from merely being present. In my experience, it is best to keep the flow of class moving, and try not to judge what anyone is or isn't getting out of it.

Embrace the unexpected with a neutral mind.

Students may exhibit surprising behavior when experiencing high emotion such as feeling excited, happy, frustrated, etc. As I began teaching yoga to a moderate/severe middle school class, one young man came up to me with his arms out to the sides, flexing his muscles to indicate he was ready to begin. I set up my mat and props and when I turned back around, he had not only taken off his shoes and socks, but all of his clothing, except for underpants. The teachers were horrified at what I would think. I just smiled outwardly and inwardly I was cracking up. Having a son who takes off his clothes when he's angry, I totally got the intense emotion leading to stripping off the clothes.

On the opposite end, students may also experience a calming of emotion and relaxation. After one particular yoga class an Autistic young man who is able to parrot language and recite entire stories, but doesn't usually engage in spontaneous language or conversation, sat on his mat, took a deep breath in and said "I feel good." His comment resonated with all of the parents in attendance, and gave hope that their kids too were experiencing this positive shift.

A Few Observations

1. Young children, and Down Syndrome students of all ages, typically have flexible joints. For instance, in Butterfly Pose many can fold forward and rest their foreheads on their feet, and actually be excited that they can smell their toes. In young children this is because flexibility is predominant in the early years, and as muscle strength develops in later childhood flexibility decreases. For students with Down Syndrome, it is important to be aware that with increased flexibility there is also typically low muscle tone, and caution should be used when stretching so as to protect the joints and not over-stretch.

2. Special needs young adults, especially females, tend to be very tight, almost locked in the pelvic region. I discussed this observation with Dr. Santokh Khalsa DC, and it is suspected this inflexible, almost constricted, pelvic region may possibly be associated with intuitive self-preservation. However, the tightness in the pelvic region adversely affects the whole spine, so I have these students work on circling the hips to stretch and align.

3. Tightness in legs, hips, and back may hinder children over 12 and adults from sitting up straight comfortably. They can be assisted in an Easy Pose posture by sitting on a folded blanket, cushion, or bolster. This provides a lift creating support for the muscles and joints.

4. The most fascinating observation I have noticed is in balance. Non-verbal students have better balance than those with speech. Those who don't have spontaneous speech can stand in tree pose like a statue, no problem. The special needs students who speak without effort are wobbly on their feet and easily fall out of balancing postures.

5. I have found many teens and young adults to be tight in the muscles through the back of the legs and hips and they do not necessarily enjoy stretching the life nerve in forward folds. This being said, I also feel it is essential to work this area in each class. (If seated on a blanket or cushion, come off of it before moving into forward folds to avoid hyperextension of the knees.) Students may extend the legs out in front of the body in the shape of a triangle, like a piece of pie, and then reach the arms up on the inhale and exhale as they reach down the legs. Or bend over one leg and gently inhale up and exhale down, then switch sides. The movement makes the stretch more tolerable than simply holding. A yoga strap, when appropriate, can be helpful in a forward fold stretch. This takes us to the next point.

6. Traditional yoga props such as straps and blocks can be turned into weapons, used on self or others. I avoid using props in special needs yoga unless I know the participants are mature enough to follow direction and use them properly.

7. What's up with the breath? I find quite often that students are not aware of their breathing, and frankly, the breath is often very shallow. I use the sense of smell, sight, and touch to teach breathing in and out, to deepen the breath, and to help teach the difference between the inhale and the exhale. I use the words breathe in and breathe out, rather than inhale and exhale because they are easier to understand.

8. It is my observation that students on the Autism Spectrum find it almost impossible to practice Cross-Crawl postures independently. That is to say, they are not easily able to use the opposite hands and feet, or arms and legs, simultaneously. Therefore, I add these types of exercises to class frequently because it activates the brain. The physical assistance of a parent is typically needed, or the exercises can be done with the mirroring of a partner. The mirror concept typically requires physical touch such as hand holding with their parent or partner in class. Some of the Cross-Crawls outlined in the chapter Cushions, Chairs and Choices can be easily mirrored. This crossing of the body is a skill not typically developed in children until after preschool age, so little ones need not master Cross-Crawls. Let them move and have fun.

"See the person, not the label." Temple Grandin (www.autismspeaks.org)

As I present information on any specific diagnosis, it is in relation to how the yoga and meditation outlined in this book affects that particular diagnosis. Or simply to relay general information that I feel is important for the reader be aware of in working with this population. The diagnosis does not define the person. I invite you to view societal verbiage such as mild, moderate, severe, high and low functioning as description not labeling.

I would like to make a special note about Down Syndrome students. It is important to be aware that their features, including eyes, nose, feet, hands and fingers are typically small. I mention these body parts because we use them in class. In some people the fingertips do not reach across the palm to touch, so performing movements such as snapping the fingers, or Kirtan Kriya meditation, which is listed below, may be challenging. Assure students ahead of time that there's no perfect posture, only each individual's personal best. It's also a good idea to keep facial tissue available and in sight, as increased attention to and use of the breath may require nose blowing. These students will rise to the occasion and try hard, although they may tire easily.

Many people I have met with Down Syndrome are fun, love life, and have big personalities, whether they are verbal or not. These kids and adults are typically not as introverted as students on the Autism Spectrum, and they are checking out what others around them are doing. Couple this with literal processing, and without any of your own doing, you may just find your class has its own personal "Posture Police." Ours is named Kimmy!

Let's get moving!

Now we are ready to tune-in and to move. As students are sitting in Easy Pose waiting to begin, you may notice protective posture: a rounded back or hunched shoulders, and an inverted heart center. A good way to correct this mediocre seated posture is to ask students to sit up tall and lift the shoulders up high, then direct them to roll the shoulders back and down letting them settle into their natural home with the heart center lifted. The spine will lengthen with this lift and roll. I demonstrate while giving directions so the movement can be copied.

I actually recommend demonstrating the entire yoga class so that students can follow along visually to practice the postures. I encourage participation by using words such as; *watch, copy, and show me*, rather than *do this or do that*. An invitation to *copy* is more empowering and well received than a direction to perform.

A *kriya* is not mandatory for family yoga class, including students of any and all ages, but I am sharing one gem that kids enjoy. The age and ability of the attendees can be taken into consideration before beginning any practice. Before moving into meditations, yoga, and themed classes outlined in this book, you can begin with a few simple warm-ups. I recommend finding a few to stick with so they become familiar. Your students will like having a routine and find comfort in the repetition.

I aim to balance a familiar warm-up routine with new and fresh yoga themes. Be aware that you may be the recipient of a possible stare down if you make changes. Even positive changes may be viewed as unwelcome. Students with an aversion to change do not hesitate to show their disapproval of minor shifts in environment, even if they can't speak. I call this communication the "death stare," and have experienced it for infractions such as opening a door or window that is typically closed, setting the lights differently, or playing a new or different version of music or mantra. You have now been forewarned.

Warm -Ups

Long Deep Breathing – Typically done in Easy Pose, breathing can be assisted by scent, possibly breathing in/smelling a natural essential oil, or a flower. When using any type of aromatherapy, it should always be an optional activity as some may be sensitive or allergic to scents. Another option is to use bean bags, books, or anything slightly weighted to observe the breath. In this case have the students lie down on the floor and place the weighted item on their bellies. They then watch and feel the item move up and down with every inhale and exhale.

Pelvic Grind – I include pelvic grind in each class because of the positive effect on the lower digestive tract. Many individuals with special needs suffer from digestive issues, and for some ASD individuals, absorption problems. Chronic constipation, loose stool, and leaky gut are all common conditions for this population, as reported by the parents of my students. The pressure and massage created by pelvic grind helps to support healthier digestion, and has been reported to ease discomfort. Although pelvic rotation puts direct stimulation on the digestive tract, the effects are subtle. In over a decade of teaching this population I have not found the effect of this exercise to send students immediately running to the restroom. However, plentiful gas may be passed, and this population doesn't typically hold back. As hard as parents and teachers may try, there seem to be no fart manners in special needs yoga, other than maybe encouragement to say "excuse me."

Head Rolls –This movement opens circulation to the brain and stimulates the thyroid, parathyroid, pineal, and pituitary glands helping to promote balance and harmony in the body.

Life Nerve Stretch – Forward folds to open the back of the legs and stretch hamstrings.

Cross -Crawls – Use the opposite hands, and feet, or arms and legs in warm ups. Crossing the midline of the body stimulates the brain, and encourages continued development. Cross- Crawls can be done mirrored with a partner by standing on the feet and holding hands to guide the use of opposite sides of the body. Encourage your partner to move with you, as if you're looking in a mirror.

Recommended *Kriya*:
Kriya to Strengthen the Aura

This set can be found in its entirety in Chapter 6 with adaptations and choices already outlined. I include this here for the outstanding effects it has on the aura.

Deep Relaxation

After completing the yoga set or themed class, I have the students come onto their backs for deep relaxation. Invite the parents to actually relax, assuring them their kids are safe and will not be leaving the room, and then be aware and watch that the kids don't wander out or off. Encourage stillness and quiet, but accept a little noise and shifting movement on the mat. Deep relaxation may last only two minutes or as long as five. Five minutes is a long deep relaxation for family style classes, especially for young children.

If available in the studio or at home, the gong can be an effective tool in relaxation. I find that this population is more sensitive to the sound vibration of the gong. When deep relaxation is accompanied by the gong, kids that are naturally noisy and wiggly settle down a bit and actually relax, while kids who are innately quiet tend to stir with subtle or overt movement. I have observed that the parents of special needs kids are typically more sensitive to the gong than non-special needs parents and adults, which suggests an over-taxed nervous system. The recommendation when it comes to utilizing the gong in special needs classes is to play softly. When students are new, I demonstrate the gong first while they are watching. With this preview they are not startled during deep relaxation.

The gong has become mainstream in recent years for its use in sound healing meditations, workshops, and special classes. For the past 40 years, in our Western culture, the gong has most commonly been found being used in Kundalini yoga classes during deep relaxation. There are three sounds that carry infinity, the human voice, the conch, and the gong.

"Although the gong has been used as an instrument in many types of world music, its most profound use lies within its singular ability to transform, heal, and elevate the spiritual seeker and seer. Today the gong has found a new audience among therapists, yoga teachers, and individuals who seek to transform themselves and others through the power of its sound."
-Mehtab Benton, *Gong Yoga, Healing and Enlightenment Through Sound* (2008)

When bringing the family class out of deep relaxation, I follow the simple wake up routine of directing the students to bring attention back to their bodies, wiggle fingers and toes, circle wrists and ankles, rub palms of the hands and soles of the feet together, stretch the arms and legs out tall, and then bring the knees into the chest and rock back and forth, up and down the spine. I eliminate the cat stretch with family yoga because the left and right twisting while using opposite arms and legs is confusing for this population. It causes more frustration than benefit.

One big benefit found in the wake-up routine comes when rubbing the palms of the hands and the soles of the feet together briskly. For clarification this is hand to hand and foot to foot, not hands to feet. This brisk rubbing actually helps to build and strengthen the aura or magnetic field. This expanded aura carries over into meditation.

Recommended Meditations:(Found at the end of the chapter.)
Bountiful, Blissful, Beautiful
Kirtan Kriya
I Am I Am with Movement
Celestial Communication
Sat Nam Wahe Guru with Movement

Set the goal for three minutes of meditation. Sometimes you'll get more, sometimes less. Let the class energy guide the length of meditation. Kids love to chant and sing and chant.

I once had a mom come in and share how helpful she found the "I Am Happy, I Am Good" meditation but had a hard time committing to it out in the open, so she would regularly practice in the shower. We got a good laugh when she reported that her husband caught her chanting and practicing the *mudra* of this meditation in the shower. *Yogable* really is about whatever works!

Closing Class – The Long Time Sun & Sat Nam

We recite and/or sign *The Long Time Sun,* using American Sign Language as outlined below, to close class with a positive blessing that is said to have Celtic origins.

May the long time sun shine upon you
All love surround you
And the pure light within you
Guide your way on

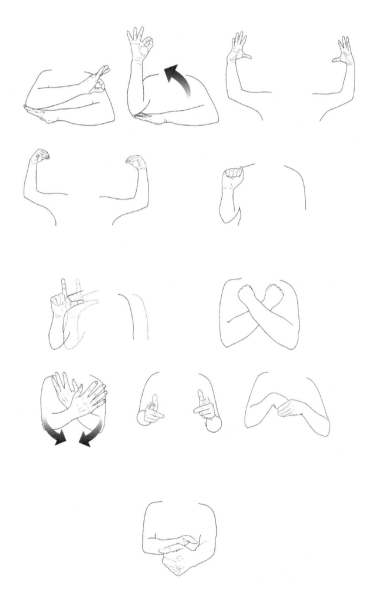

The ending mantra *Sat Nam* can cause confusion and humor when defining it to children. At one time in my teaching career, I tried to give the literal definition to kids, "Truth is my identity." Even with further explanation, the kids thought my name was "Miss Truth" and started calling me such. I simply tell the kids and family classes that *Sat Nam* stands for our own truth and honesty. It's similar to using *Namaste* found in hatha yoga practice.

Additional insights and tips:

1. I want to make a special note on balance here. As I mentioned, individuals who are non-verbal or who do not have spontaneous speech demonstrate better balance in yoga postures, whereas individuals who are verbal struggle more with balance. Reverend Bruyere describes those on the Autism Spectrum Disorder without the use of verbal language as being "in their bodies," energetically connected to their legs, and therefore better at balance. Those on the spectrum with speech are observed to be concentrated energetically up in their heads, lacking full energetic connection to their bodies and legs, and therefore they struggle with balancing postures. This energetic relationship with the body has a profoundly physical implication and response. Basically, balance is affected by the energetic state of each student, which provides the experience of being in the body and legs, or not. Jumping, positioning the feet in yoga posture, and moving the feet on the floor builds the aura around the legs and the feeling of being in the body.

2. The lymphatic system in the body does not have its own pump. This system relies on the individual to move and breathe in order to circulate lymph to keep the body clean on the inside. Many of our special students engage in stimming behaviors such as flapping, clapping, or repetitive movement with the hands and arms. It is my observation that this movement stays in fairly close to body, or is extended out to the sides of the body, with almost zero full arm extension up over the head. Utilizing postures such as Bird Pose, Sun Salutes, and Spinal Twist with an arm stretch helps to stimulate the lymphatic system.

3. I already made a note on digestion in relation to pelvic rotation exercise, but want to add additional comments. Pelvic grind also opens energy in the lower spine, increases flexibility, and massages the liver. Long deep breathing is also helpful for proper digestion and elimination.

4. Anyone need tips for sleep??
   - First, turn your bed so that it runs east to west. This will ensure that the body is least disturbed by the earth's magnetic pull during sleep. For best results place the head at the east end of the bed.
   - Develop a bedtime routine that allows for a quieting and slowing of the body 30 minutes before getting into bed. Clean the teeth, mouth and the inside of the nose.
   - Drink a bit of water so you don't get dehydrated at night.
   - Falling asleep is best achieved when the breath is moving predominantly through the left nostril. To help achieve this you can lie on the right side of the body to encourage the left nostril to open. If the left nostril is mostly plugged up, gently close the right nostril with one of the fingers of the right hand and begin breathing in and out of the left nostril for a few minutes.

Utilize these few yogic tips as desired. They work for all ages and abilities!

Reported Benefits and Testimonial:
- Acceptance, and the experience of a friendly, welcoming and safe class
- Decreased anxiety
- Appreciation for an activity kids and parents can do together
- Fun
- Improved sleep
- Relaxation
- The body feels better with movement
- Relief from stress, upset and tension
- Smiling children
- Increased body and spatial awareness
- Increased ability to attend to tasks for longer periods
- Increased focus by using techniques outside of the class setting

"My daughter and I have been attending a special needs yoga class for over 3 years. Each class has a theme, as well as regular activities that bring the consistency that kids need. Both my daughter and I benefit physically and mentally from yoga. We feel welcome, special and peaceful. We never miss a class."

– Mary W.

"My son and I love coming to special needs yoga class. It has helped in so many ways such as increased relaxation, reduced anxiety, improved imitation skills, and I see a smile on my son's face. Even my son's teachers have noticed positive changes in his mood after going to yoga class. We look forward to it every week."

-Jackie E.

"I love the fact that we are encouraged to do the movements that are comfortable for us and we perform at our ability...no pressure to do what everyone else is doing. The environment is calm, peaceful, and it totally takes you to another place! There is a sense of accomplishment and finally getting that self-care that is needed."

- Denise E.

Kriya and Meditations

Kriya to Strengthen the Aura
Kriya to Strengthen the Aura is found at the end of Chapter 6, and may be taught with the given adaptations to kids or in a family class.

<u>Bountiful, Blissful, and Beautiful</u>

Bountiful am I, Blissful am I, Beautiful am I is an uplifting affirmation. Although there is no prescribed meditation for this song, I find it to be a good fit for family and kids yoga classes. I have the students sing or recite as described below.

Sit in Easy Pose. Place the hands, one on top of the other, on the center of the chest, the Heart Center. Close the eyes and sing the for 1 to 7 minutes. An alternate posture is to place the hands on the knees in Gyan Mudra. Remind students they are claiming and developing their bounty, bliss and beauty.

I ask the kids what each of these words mean, and then may assist with a translation along the lines of "*I have more than enough, I am happy, I am beautiful.*" I invite the kids to be thankful for what they have in their own lives. For example, bountiful may be described as having plenty of food on your dinner plate.

Bountiful am I, Blissful am I, Beautiful am I

Kirtan Kriya Meditation

This meditation has already been outlined in its entirety in a Chapter 6. It is an amazing practice for kids to work on mental coordination and clarity.

Follow the basic directions, without worrying about focus and visualization. Some of the students will be able to close their eyes and chant and some will need to keep the eyes open to follow along and copy the leader.

Chant the mantra *Saa Taa Naa Maa* while pressing the corresponding fingers together.

30 seconds aloud
30 seconds whisper
1 minute silent
30 seconds whisper
30 seconds aloud

Sit quietly for a few breaths. Then inhale, stretch the arms overhead and shake. Relax. This takes Kirtan Kriya to just slightly over 3 minutes.

An alternative to changing the volume of the voice is to keep the mantra and movement going aloud for 1 to 3 minutes.

A special note about students with Down Syndrome and Kirtan Kriya – as features of Down Syndrome individuals are small, including hands and feet, the thumb and little finger may not reach across the palm to touch. Let students know this is okay and encourage them to do the best they can with the fingertips that do touch.

I'd like to share a true, sweet story about *Kirtan Kriya* and the pediatric neurology clinic. My son's yearly visits to the neurologist typically include a series of tests. One such test is to touch each of the fingertips, in succession, to the tip of the thumb. The first time my son was asked to do this, he jumped right in singing *Saa Taa Naa Maa* as he pressed his fingers together. Finally, a test he could ace! His doctor looked a bit perplexed until I explained it's a yoga meditation song. Neurology tests this finger movement/ability because it is connected to brain function.

I Am, I Am

Begin with the hands crossed over the heart center, one on top of the other; either hand on top is okay. In this position chant the first *"I AM."* Then stretch the arms over the head at a sixty-degree angle, in the shape of a "V" for victory, and chant the second *"I AM."* Continue singing and alternating hands from the heart center to extended over the head for 1 to 3 minutes. To end, inhale deeply, exhale, and relax.

Celestial Communication

Sit in Easy Pose. Repeat the words below with the outlined Celestial Communication hand and arm movements as given by Hari Kirn Kaur Khalsa.

I am Happy, I am Good

Sat Nam, Sat Nam, Sat Nam Ji – *Sat Nam* means truth is my identity.

Wahe Guru Wahe Guru Wahe Guru Ji – *Wahe Guru* is the experience of moving from darkness to light. *Ji* is an affectionate, yet respectful term for the soul.

Continue singing for 1 to 5 minutes. This is by far the most popular meditation for kids. My students love it, both adults and children of all ages and abilities. We practice in a style of movement called Celestial Communication, as given by Hari Kirn Kaur Khalsa, wherein *mudra* (hand position) and mantra (chanting) are linked.

I am Happy, I am Good
I am Happy, I am Good
Shake the index fingers up and down for both repetitions.
Sat Nam, Sat Nam, Sat Nam Ji
Place the hands in prayer pose and move up the body; navel center, heart center, and forehead on the *Sat Nams*, then end in Ji with the hands open over the head.
Wahe Guru, Wahe Guru, Wahe Guru Ji
With the arms over the head begin to circle the hands at the wrists and direct this circling movement down in front of the body on the *Wahe Gurus*. End at *Ji* with the palms up and knees width apart.

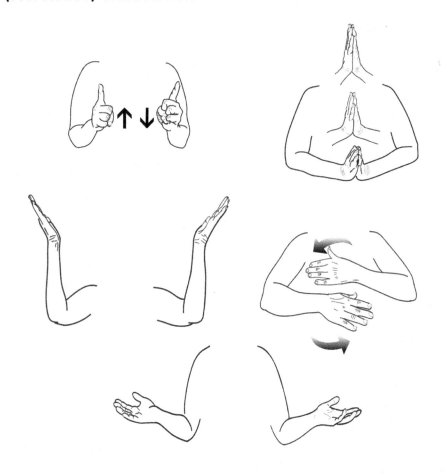

"Celestial Communication is a form of meditation where the body becomes the instrument to play the sound current. Sit still, tune in, and sing with your favorite uplifting music while moving the arms and upper body. Experience a meditative state of rising spirit and deep relaxation through this simple and universal practice."

– Hari Kirn Kaur Khalsa (2020)

Additional Comment:

On occasion students may communicate through ASL, or American Sign Language. One of the young men in my class uses rudimentary sign language to communicate. When we practice meditations using Celestial Communication movement, he uses ASL for the words he knows, and I'm just sure he thinks I'm an idiot for not getting it right. He's participating at a level that is comfortable for him, and I don't make corrections. There is no need to make anyone understand the concept of Celestial Communication, simply allow for individual communication, movement, and joy.

Sat Nam Wahe Guru

Sit in Easy Pose with a straight spine. Hands are in Gyan Mudra (the tip of the thumb and the tip of the index fingers together.) Say the mantra out loud and alternately circle the arms, one at a time, up and over the head and down in back. The sweeping motion may extend down and behind the head, neck, or even the back based on flexibility of the shoulders. One arm up and over the head on the first *Sat Nam*, the opposite arm goes up and over on the second *Sat Nam*, then repeat alternate arm circles with each *Wahe Guru*. The sweeping arm movement not only builds the aura, but actually pulls concentrated energy over the head, directing and smoothing it down the spine helping to create expanded auric coverage. This fortifies the protective capacities of the aura. This rhythm of the movement can easily be followed with the song included on the accompanying soundtrack. Continue for 2-5 minutes. Inhale, stretch, twist, and exhale.

Sat Nam, Sat Nam, Wahe Guru, Wahe Guru

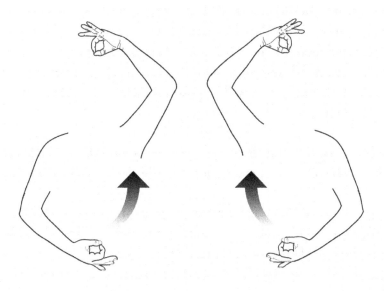

Additional comment:

This is another movement with song that is both fun and beneficial for students of all ages. I enjoy watching my students practice this meditation to observe all of the individual interpretations of my physical example. Some students close their eyes while they swing their arms in wide circles, their faces held in complete and utter peace and bliss. Others keep the eyes open and circle arms close to the body, skimming over the head in an almost shy manner. I have included this movement for the effect on the aura.

9

Family Fun and Function for All

"When I say it's you I like, I'm talking about that part of you that knows that life is far more than anything you can ever see or hear or touch. That deep part of you that allows you to stand for those things without which humankind cannot survive. Love that conquers hate, peace that rises triumphant over war, and justice that proves more powerful than greed."

- Fred Rogers (2002)

Traditional *kriyas* can benefit children and those with special needs, however they are not a requirement to have an amazing class experience. *Kriyas* can be technical, precise, and too demanding for this population. My goal is simply to get these students moving and meditating in ways that benefit body, mind, and spirit, while having fun. This chapter is full of outlines for family style classes with themes or topics. The postures included in this chapter are drawn from the large pool of yoga branches, and are not *kriyas*.

The suggested class outline is to tune in with *Ong Namo, Guru Dev Namo* before beginning the yoga practice, followed by relaxation, meditation and the closing *Long Time Sun* song.

Remember if you find yourself teaching for a group or organization that is either not comfortable with mantra, or requests no chanting be included in the class, tuning in can be done mentally and/or the class may be provided space to get ready for yoga by taking 3 deep breaths in place of tuning in with mantra. This may also hold true if the mantra does not resonate personally with the instructor. What's important is to give time and peaceful energy to move into the practice with ease.

It may be helpful to direct students to shake out and wiggle between exercises, especially after a high energy posture. This is good for kids and parents. When practicing the themed yoga classes, it may also be helpful to direct kids to end each posture with a deep breath in through the nose and out through the mouth. It helps to distinguish inhale and exhale, and to transition to the next posture.

When giving instruction during a family or children's yoga class it is best to avoid phrasing directions in the form of a question. Give clear, concrete direction. For example, if teaching a class where students take turns picking posture cards or animals, you can simply let them know it is their turn to pick rather than asking if they want to pick a card. If they decline that is fine, but questions can be too much to process in an already sensory filled activity.

Deep relaxation times will vary depending on age, developmental functioning, and the group dynamics. In general, 2 minutes is a good place to start. This can be shortened if needed, or extended to five minutes. I use the word deep relaxation, but this may be a rustling, noisy time for some even though they are relaxing.

Meditation is highly encouraged! Whether simply focusing on a few slow, quiet breaths, or practicing one of the meditations outlined in the previous chapter, please feel free to add any meditation to themed classes.

Themed Classes and Ideas:

I am presenting plenty of postures in each of the following themed classes for thirty to forty-five minute classes when including relaxation and meditation. Each posture is done to tolerance, and class flows freely. There is no need to time one-to-three minutes for each posture. Please feel free to take postures out or add additional postures so that the timing is right for your individual class or practice. Some of these themes can even be split up into two or more sessions.

Surprise Postures – Fill a bag or basket with stuffed animals, squishy animals, and hard figurines, all of which will have a corresponding yoga pose. Have the students take turns pulling an item out of the bag and then the class does the yoga pose. Pick a variety of textures to place in the bag for a tactile experience. For challenge and surprise, you can ask students to reach in and pull out an object without peeking, either by closing the eyes or looking in another direction.

Animal Cards – Fill an envelope or small bag with cards that have a picture of an animal on them. Make sure the animals you choose have a corresponding yoga pose. Invite students to take turns pulling a card and then the class does the animal yoga posture on the card. You can purchase your yoga cards by going to an educational or craft store and buying a pack of animal cards, or there are many premade decks of yoga postures for kids to be found online. If you are an artist, you can create your own animal cards. You can even have your students draw and color animals on blank cards! By mounting the animal card to a piece of card stock paper, you can write the benefits of the posture on the back. In classes with kids who are at the appropriate reading level, they can read the back of the card and share what the class is working on in each posture.

The following list of animal postures are utilized throughout family and/or kid's classes. Themed classes may include description, rather than illustration, for simple hand/arm movements or breath given within the class outline.

List of Animal Postures:

Ant - Come on to knees and elbows and walk around the room like ants.

Armadillo - Lie on your back and hug the knee into the chest and rock up and down along the spine. You can alternate the name of this movement to be a tumbleweed, avalanche, or anything that fits into your class.

Bear – This is like down-dog, but the legs are as wide as your mat with the knees slightly bent.

Bee Breath – In Easy Pose, inhale through the nose and exhale through the nose with a hum. You can place the hands on the chest to feel the vibration of the lungs. In a group this breath sounds like a swarm of bees.

Bird – Sit or stand and let the arms drop down to each side, then inhale arms out and up like bird wings and exhale back down.

Bug - Lie on the back, bend knees in toward shoulders, feet up toward the ceiling. From here reach up and hold on to the back of the thighs or the bottom of the feet. Good for sciatic nerve, hips, and lower back. We affectionately call this one "Mom's Choice."

Bunny – See Kangaroo and then make smaller hops.

Butterfly – Sit up tall with the bottom of the feet touching. Hold on to the ankles and gently move the knees up and down like butterfly wings.

Camel Pose – Stand on the knees and reach the arms back behind toward the heels. Chest up and head gently back. Support with arms at the lower back if needed.

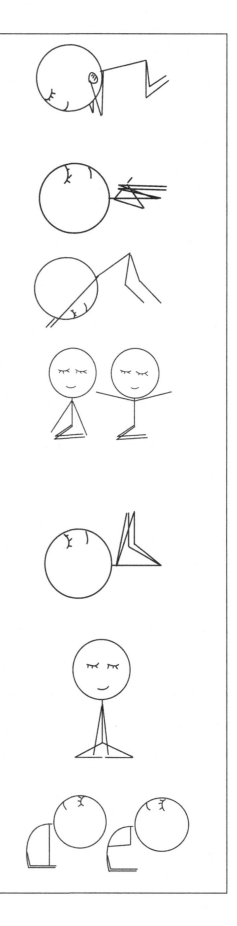

Camel Ride – Follow instructions for Spinal Flex.

Cobra – Lie on the belly and place the hands under the shoulders. Inhale and as you exhale push up into a backbend.

Cat-Cow – On the hands and knees begin flexing the spine up and down.

Crab - Come up on feet and hands, face up, and walk around like a crab.

Cricket – Lying on the back bring the palms of the hands together, and the bottom of the feet together and rub briskly.

Crow Squat– Come into a deep squat with the hands in prayer pose at the heart or extended out in front of the body.

Dolphin – Another pose that starts in down-dog. From down-dog pose come down on the elbows with fingers interlaced as you walk the feet in closer to the body, as the crown of the head faces toward the ground, creating a dolphin dive.

Donkey Kicks – Start in down-dog, like a triangle, then kick legs up and out alternately, or both at once.

Down Dog – in Kundalini Yoga, we call this Triangle Pose.

Eagle – Stand in a slight squat and cross arms & legs around each other, and switch sides.

Elephant Walk - Fold forward half way down, make a trunk with the arms and march around the room. Swing your trunk (arms) and stomp the feet to connect with the earth.

Fish – Lie on the back with the legs extended. Come up on to the elbows, lifting the heart up toward the sky, and gently drop the head back.

Flamingo - Stand on one leg for balance.

Frog Stretch – On elbows and knees, spread the knees apart to stretch the inner leg.

Gorilla – Stand with the feet hip distance and fold forward placing the hands, palms up, under the toes and feet. Bend the knees as needed to accommodate arms.

Horse – Stand up and bring your hands and feet to the floor, face down, lift opposite hands and feet in a march or run.

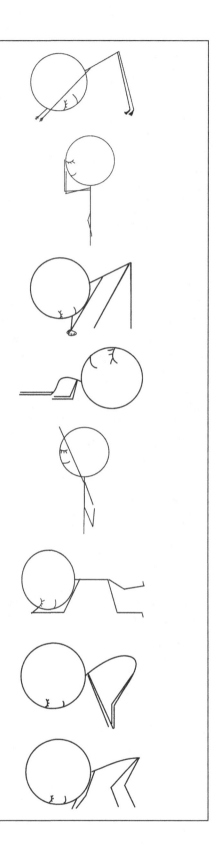

Kangaroo – Stand up with bent elbows, hands relaxed, knees bent and hop on both feet like a kangaroo.

Lion Breath – Take one or two powerful sniffs in through the nose, one strong exhale out through the open mouth while sticking out your tongue. This can be done sitting on the heels with the hands on the floor in front of knees, or seated in Easy Pose.

Lizard – Take a high or low lunge while looking forward, with both hands on the inside of the front foot. An alternate is to do push-ups like lizards do while basking in the sun.

Monkey – Stand with feet hip distance and fold forward placing the hands on the shins and then flatten the back and raise the head to look forward.

Mouse – Come in to baby pose, and stick out the hands out in front like little feet.

Owl – Sitting or standing turn the head from side to side like shaking the head no, but move slowly.

Penguin - Stand on the knees with arms out tight by the sides for balance then walk around the room on the knees with the feet lifted off of the floor.

Praying Mantis - Perform any variation of Prayer Pose; classic, *Gurupranam*, or reverse prayer.

Spider – Come into a full squat as shown in Crow Pose. Hands can rest down on the floor between the legs, with fingers spread wide to mimic the legs of a spider.

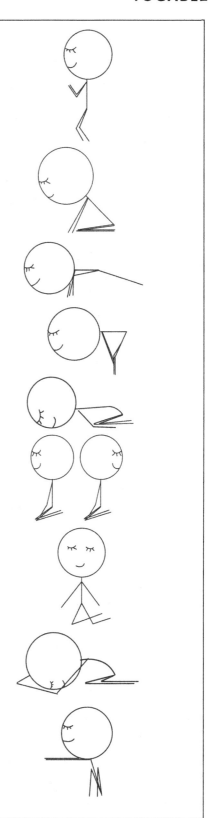

Beach Yoga

<u>Sponge breath</u> – Ask the students to breathe in big, expanding their lungs like a sponge, then breathe out deflating the sponge. I actually bring in a soft sponge to squeeze for demonstration.

<u>Waves-</u> Feet together as in butterfly pose, then rock from side to side. This posture helps balance the hormones.

<u>Penguin –</u> Come up standing on the knees, arms down straight and at an angle like penguin wings, lift the feet off of the floor and walk around the room on the knees. Good for balance.

<u>Fish Pose</u> – Gentle version, legs out, propped up on the elbows, head tilted back if neck allows.

<u>Sting Ray Arms</u> – Extend the arms out to the side and flap the arms up and down loosely, like a sting ray swimming through the sea.

<u>Shark Arms</u> – One arm up at a sixty- degree angle, palm facing down, one arm down at a sixty-degree angle, palm facing up. Move arms so that the palms meet like a shark biting. After ten repetitions, switch arms and repeat.

<u>Crab Walk</u> – Basically just as in PE class. Come up on the hands and the knees with the front of the body facing up, bottom slightly dropped toward the ground, and walk around forward, backward, side to side.

Swimming – Come on to the stomach, extend the arms out in front along the ground, palms down. Lift the legs and the arms and move them up and down in a swimming motion. (I have been known to put the theme song to *Jaws* on during this posture, it keeps the grown-ups alert!).

Rock Pose – Moving up on to the beach, we sit on the heels in rock pose. Good for digestion.

Tree Pose – Come on to the feet for tree pose. Use the wall for balance if needed.

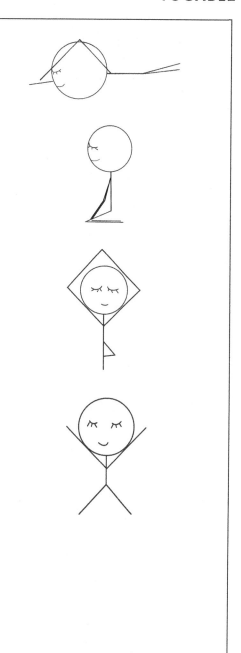

Sun Pose – Stand with the feet in a wide stance. Raise the arms above the head at the same distance as the feet.

Sea Shells – Bring along a large shell to pass around the class and ask the students to hold it up to their ear to see if they can hear the ocean. Alternately bring along enough small shells for each student to hold during meditation. They can keep the shells to remind them of their meditation experience.

Sleeping Starfish – An alternate name for Corpse Pose: *savasana*, or deep relaxation. Lie out on the ground, face up, like a starfish.

Camping Trip Yoga

Mountain Pose- Stand tall, arms at sides, palms forward.

Set up Tent – Come into Down-Dog like the shape of a tent.

Hike into the woods – Yogi March around the room.

Bear Pose – Like triangle (Down-dog) but with legs the width of the mat with knees slightly bent.

Fish Pose – Lie on the back, come up on elbows and lift the chest up while dropping the head back.

Cobra Pose – This can represent any kind of snake.

Crickets – Lie on the back and rub hands and feet together. This strengthens the aura.

Then set up for a campfire – bring a lantern or flashlight and sit in a circle around the fire. I cover the lantern with colored scarves for ambiance.

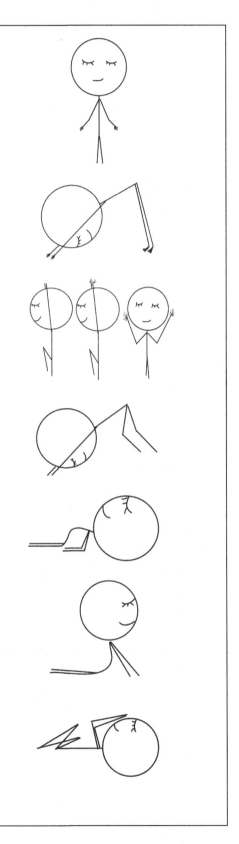

Fire – <u>Snap the fingers</u>, all of the fingers, like a crackling, popping fire. This is good for stimulating the nerve endings of the fingers that connect to the brain.

<u>Rub Palms together</u> – Create some warmth and get cozy by the fire, while encouraging communication between the hemispheres of the brain and promoting calmness of mind.

Make S'mores – Extend arms out toward the imaginary fire and <u>rotate the wrists,</u> first in one direction and then the other. Then blow on the s'mores to cool.

Oops, we made a mess. First, we'll clean up and then deal with… the ants!

<u>Move the tongue around the mouth and over the teeth in circles.</u> Move the tongue in both directions pretending to clean away the sticky marshmallow from the s'mores.

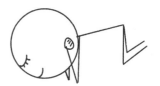

<u>Ant Pose</u>- Come on to the stomach, then up on to the knees and elbows and walk around the room like ants.

Roll up in your sleeping bags – <u>Have the kids lie across their mats at one end and parents roll them up in the mat, like being rolled up in a sleeping bag.</u> Repeat this roll up a couple of times, and then switch and let the kids roll up the parents. The pressure of this roll can be calming and grounding, particularly for students with ASD.

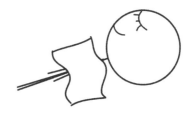

<u>Coyote Howl</u>- Make a howling noise like a coyote.

<u>Snore</u> – Pretend to snore as you move into deep relaxation. This helps to release anger and irritation.

Desert Trip Yoga

<u>Rock Pose</u> – Sit on the heels then use a <u>whistle breath</u> to create the howling wind of the desert. Inhale and exhale through the mouth making a whistling sound. For those who can't whistle, just blow. It all comes together to make a windy sound.

<u>Camel Ride</u> – Spinal Flex
<u>Camel Pose</u>
<u>Lizard Pose</u>

<u>Cobra Pose</u> – Have the kids take a breath in while on the belly and when they lift up into cobra pose hiss like a snake. Come back down for a new breath and repeat 3 times. (I remind the front row that there are no actual spitting cobras in class, only dry hissing. This is no joke!)

<u>Bird</u> – Lift the arms up over the head touching the back of the hands together on the inhale and exhale arms down to the sides.

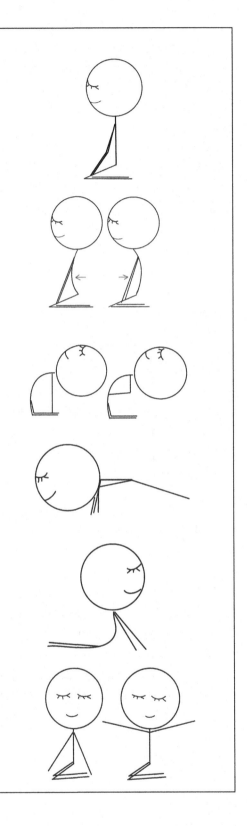

<u>Spinal Twist</u> – Sit up in the shape of a cactus, arms out to the side, elbows bent with hands up in Gyan mudra, then twist side to side.

<u>Rock back and forth on the spine</u> – Imagine you are tumbleweed rolling across the desert. (I sometimes call this armadillo.)

<u>Bug Pose</u>
<u>Baby Pose</u> – Come into baby pose and pretend to be a little mouse or rodent.

For a tactile experience you can bring in rubber snakes, lizards, and bugs for students to touch and feel, or place rocks in their hands during deep relaxation for grounding. Just make sure that you know your student's maturity level before handing out rocks, as you don't want any thrown during deep relaxation.

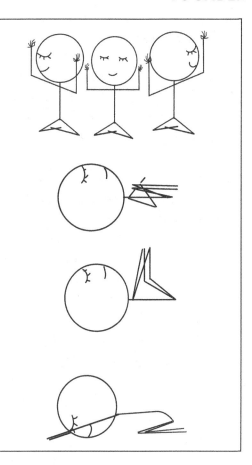

Winter Yoga

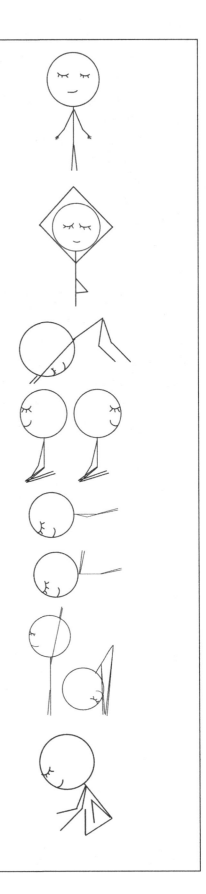

Dragon Breath – Take 3 to 4 (choose and give direction for 3 or 4, rather than letting the students decide) sniffs in through the nose, then one big exhale through the mouth with the tongue sticking out.

Mountain Pose – Stand tall with feet under the hips. Arms are down by the hips with the palms facing forward.

Tree Pose – Come into tree pose, both sides.

After the posture, I pass around pine cones and ask each student how the pine cones feel and what they smell like. If I have collected enough pine cones, I send one home with each student along with directions on how to make a bird feeder. (Spread almond butter on the pine cone, roll it in bird seed, hang it in a tree).

Bear Pose

Owl Pose – Standing or sitting, turn the head slowly from side to side.

Sled Pose – Actually Locust Pose. Lie on the belly with arms extended out to the front and the legs extended out to the back of the body, then lift arms and legs up off the ground while pretending to sled down a snowy mountain.

Whistle Breath- Imitate the wind

Snowy Forward Folds – Stand up and inhale arms up over the head, fold forward on the exhale and wiggle the fingers gently to imitate falling snow. Continue moving up and down.

Thunder – Sit in Easy Pose and beat the ground in front of you with both hands – this helps to release anger and irritation.

Spring Yoga

Aromatherapy for Focus – Pass around any uplifting fragrance such as an essential oil orange & peppermint blend, a rose or other fragrant flower (optional).

Bee Breath – Take a deep breath in and hum it out, vibrating in the lungs. The group will sound like a hive of bees. This is a gentle and safe way for kids to use *pranayam* and strengthen the lungs.

Butterfly Pose

Puffy Clouds – Stand on the feet, squat down, then stand up and raise arms in a circle over the head like a big cloud. Repeat several times.

Sun Salute with Rain Showers – Stand on the feet and inhale arms up saluting the sun, then fold forward and wiggle the fingers like rain coming down. Rain can be gentle or powerful based on the movement of the fingers.

Rain Stick – Bring in a rain stick, or have each student make a rain stick, and let each student move the rain stick to make noise. (This is optional. Directions for making rain sticks in class follows later in this chapter.)

Blooming Flower – St in rock pose, inhale up onto the knees raising the arms up and out at a sixty-degree angle, then bow down with hands on the floor in front of the knees. Continue to come up like a flower blooming, and back down like a seed.

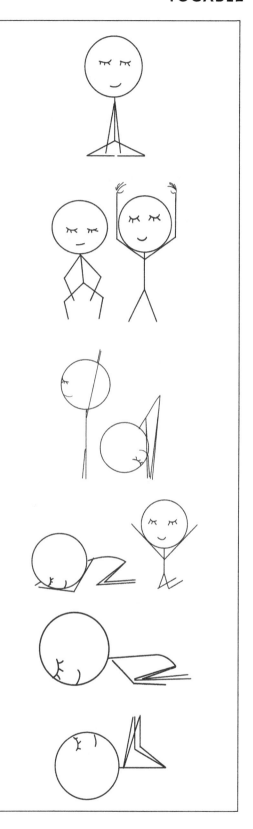

<u>Baby Pose</u> – Spring is the season of new birth!
<u>Bug Pose</u>
<u>Bunnies</u> – Hop around the room like a bunny.

<u>Dancing</u> – Put on uplifting music or mantra and dance.

If your space permits, you can facilitate a Spring activity where the kids plant their own flower or vegetable seeds in a small pot of soil. They can take the pots home and watch them grow. An alternative is to hand out seeds to plant as an at home activity.

Another fun Spring Equinox activity is to bring leaves, collected from the ground, and give one to each class participant. Invite students to write one positive affirmation word on the leaf, meditate on the leaf, and then return the leaf to nature after class. Maybe someone else will find your affirmation.

Summer Picnic Yoga

<u>Sun Salute</u>- Forward folds

<u>Sun Pose</u>- Stand with legs wide and stretch arms up and out wide, like a sun.

<u>Tree Pose</u>

<u>Bird Arms</u>

<u>Down-dog Pose</u>

<u>Butterfly Pose</u>

<u>Table Pose</u> – Become the picnic table by coming on to the hands and knees with a neutral spine.

<u>Chair Pose</u> – Pretend to sit around the picnic table.

<u>Veggie Dog Roll</u> – Lie across mat and roll up like a veggie dog, parents may use pressure with hands to imitate putting on condiments.

<u>Ants</u> – Come on to knees and elbows and walk around the room like ants.

<u>Bicycling</u> – Lie on the back and circle the legs like riding a bike. This can be done solo or with a parent partner. Try cycling the pretend bike in both directions.

<u>Lemonade to drink at the end of class</u> – For smell & taste.

(One of the best snacks for kids with allergies and food issues is lemonade and graham crackers, however always check with the parent or guardian before serving snacks.)

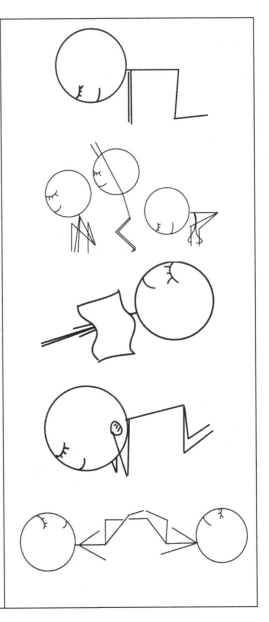

Farm Yoga

<u>Cat- Cow Pose</u> – Imagine the barn cats sneaking in to steal milk from the cows.

<u>Mouse Pose</u> – Come into Baby Pose with the hands palms down in front of the shoulders.

<u>Down Dog Pose</u> – Because well, dogs work on the farm.

<u>Donkey Pose</u> – In Triangle Pose try to kick the legs out behind you, one at a time or for more challenge try both at the same time.

<u>Horse Pose</u> – Standing on the hands and the feet, legs slightly bent, begin lifting the opposite hand and foot off the ground at the same time, like a horse trotting.

<u>Bird Pose</u>

<u>Scarecrow Pose</u> – stand up and lift the arms out to the sides, elbows bent, hands up in *gyan mudra* and twist side to side. You're a scarecrow keeping the crops safe from the birds.

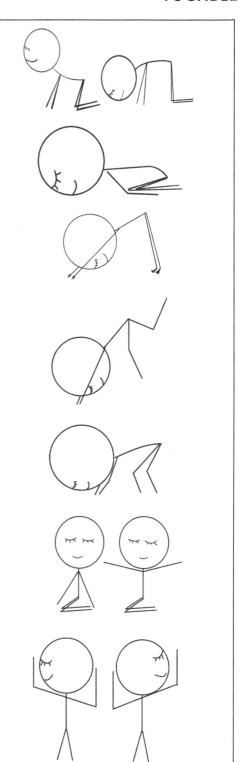

Swaying Cornfield –Stand on the feet lift the arms up in the air, keep the arms loose and pretend you're a field of corn stalks as you sway from side to side and back and forth in the wind.

Tree Pose – Because food grows on trees, *duh*!

Smelling or Sensory Activity – This is a great time to bring in fruits or vegetables to pass around for the students to touch and feel the texture, and also to smell, or even eat at the end of class.

Table Pose – Pretend you're a table and we're going eat what we've harvested.

Chair Pose – Pull a chair up to the table to eat. Check out the variety of Chair Poses available and pick the one that is right for your body.

Things That Fly Yoga

This is an example of a wonderful set for those in wheelchairs, chairs, or groups of kids with a variety of abilities. I will outline the modified poses below, but both modified and original postures may be practiced in a mixed ability class. Original postures are illustrated. Follow directions for adaptations.

Hot Air Balloon – This is done with a breathing technique called Balloon Breath. Begin with the arms relaxed at the side. Inhale through the nose and lift the arms up in a circle until the hands meet over the head. Exhale through the mouth as the arms float down. Repeat 3-4 times. Balloon Breath is accredited to childrensyoga.com.

Bird Arms – After practicing 5-10 Bird Arm repetitions, pause to ask students what type of bird is their favorite.

Eagle Arms – Like Eagle Pose, but use the arms only.

Owl Pose – Turn the head from side to side.

Helicopter – Extend the arms out to the side and twist left and right imitating the circular movement of helicopter blades.

Airplane – Extend the arms straight out to the sides, palms facing down. Hold this arm posture while leaning forward with a straight spine.

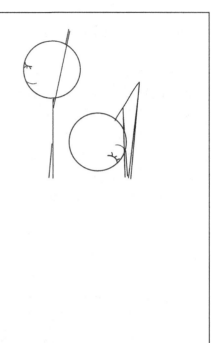

Wheel Pose – Not the backbend, but an alternate pose like the wheels found on an airplane. Bring the forearms in front of the body and circle the wrists around each other. Try going fast and slow, forward and backward.

Swan Dive (a type of forward fold) – Spread the knees apart to make space between each leg. Lift the arms up and then dive down into a forward fold and let the body and arms hang between the legs. Repeat the forward folds. Inhale up and exhale down.

Kirtan Kriya Meditation – Chant Sa Ta Na Ma while pressing finger tips together as outlined in Chapter 6.

Use these topics and more, along with postures already listed, to create your own class. Some additional ideas may include:

Jungle Cruise Yoga
Neighborhood Yoga
Weather Themed Yoga

Road Trip, Road Trip! Road Trip Yoga through the United States

This topic can cover 4-6 weeks of classes. It is helpful to purchase a large map of the United States, or a children's puzzle of the United States. The students pick out a puzzle piece (state), or point to a state on the map and then the class does the corresponding posture listed below. If you're using a puzzle you can leave time for the class to put the puzzle together at the end of the series. Please keep in mind it was a creative stretch to come up with postures to pair with each of the states!

Don't have a puzzle or map? Then you choose eight-to-ten state postures and create your own class road trip. This same concept can be done for any city, state, country, continent, or even a trip around the world! For example, Windmills for the Netherlands, Down Dog for the pyramids of Egypt, and Cobra Pose for India. You get the idea!

State Postures

Alabama - <u>Heart Breath</u> for the Heart of Dixie. Breathe in through the nose and imagine breathing out through the center of the chest, the heart center. The exhale actually comes back out the nose, but feel the heart center expand.

Alaska - <u>Bear Pose</u>

Arizona - <u>Standing cactus twist</u> for this big desert state.

Arkansas – <u>Eagle Pose</u> for the eagle on the state seal.

California - <u>Bridge Pose</u> in honor of the famous Golden Gate Bridge.

Colorado - <u>Rock Pose</u> in honor of The Rocky Mountains known as "The Rockies."

Connecticut - <u>Bicycle Pose</u>. Move the legs in a bicycle motion, solo or with a partner all the way across the state. Try going forward and backward with your cycling motion.

Delaware - <u>Criss-Cross arms or legs</u>. Cross the Delaware River by using your limbs.

Florida - Orange is the state fruit. The teacher or student can bring oranges to class to use as focus for meditation, to smell and/or to eat.

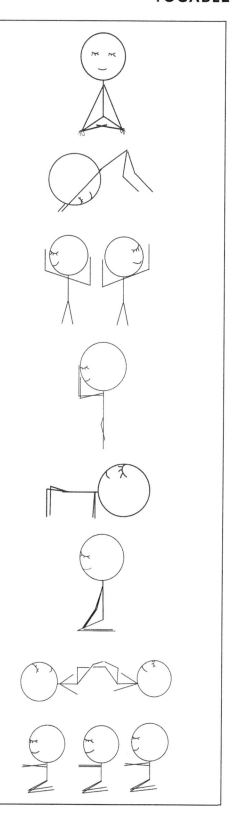

Georgia - Peach Pie stretch for the "Peach State." Sit with legs extended out to each side with the legs in the shape of a piece of pie, alternately stretch down to each side in a <u>Forward Fold</u>. Inhale up to center, exhale down over each leg.

Hawaii - <u>Sun Salutation</u> to salute the beautiful sun. Practice a simple standing forward fold, inhale up and exhale down.

Idaho - <u>Bird Arms</u> to fly like the state bird, the Mountain Bluebird.

Illinois - Powerful forward fold for Chicago, also known as the "Windy City." <u>Standing Forward Fold</u> up and down with a Powerful breath in and out through the mouth like the wind.

Indiana - <u>Run in place</u>. The first Indianapolis 500 was held here.

Try run as fast, like a race car.

Iowa - <u>Down-dog</u> in honor of dogs helping farmers.

Kansas - <u>Feet tap</u> because there's no place like home! (From *The Wizard of Oz*) Good for detoxing the body. Lie down on the back with the sides of the feet together, keeping the heels together tap the sides of the upper feet and big toes together.

Kentucky - <u>Horse Pose</u> for the famous horse race, The Kentucky Derby.

Louisiana - <u>Yogi March</u> for Mardi Gras! March in place.
Beads are optional.

Maine - <u>Tree Pose</u>. Ninety percent of the state of Maine is covered in trees and is still undeveloped forest.

Maryland - <u>Crab Walk</u> for the state's famous Blue Crab.

Massachusetts - <u>Chair Pose</u>. Imagine you are sitting down to tea in the big city of Boston.

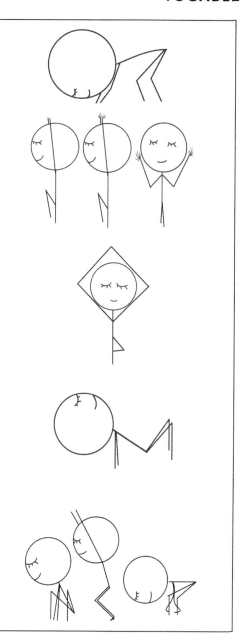

Michigan - <u>Wheel Pose</u> because Detroit is the "Motor City" capital of the U.S. An alternate to full wheel pose is to bring the forearms in front of the body and circle the wrists around each other.

Minnesota - <u>Boat Pose</u> for the "Land of 10,000 Lakes." Yes, there are over 10,000 lakes in this state!

Mississippi - <u>Frog Stretch</u>. Pretend you can hear the frogs in the bayou, or even make your own frog noises.

Missouri - <u>Bee Breath</u> is a safe breath for kids, and good for strengthening the lungs. Inhale deeply and exhale in a hum. The room will sound like a bee hive. The bee is Missouri's state insect.

Montana - <u>Plow Pose</u> to get through the blizzards and snow.

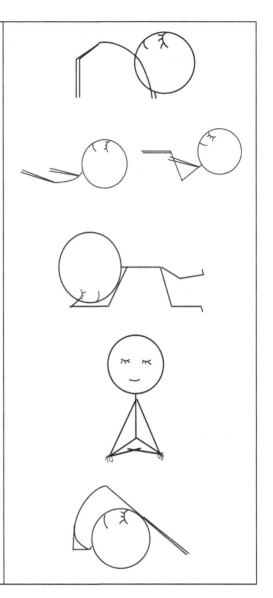

Nebraska - Swaying Corn Fields. Stand on the feet, raise arms in the air and <u>sway side to side and back and forth</u> like corn stalks blowing in the wind.

Nevada - Slot machine arms - Reach out alternate arms with open hands and pull back in with the hands coming into fists. This looks like a <u>swimming motion</u>, but we're imitating playing old school slot machines in Las Vegas. Add the mantra Sa Ta Na Ma with each arm movement.

New Hampshire - The ninth state to join the Union. Do nine bunny hops, or 9 repetitions of any other posture of choice.

New Jersey - Train Whistle. Imagine you are in a train station and practice <u>whistle breath</u>. See if you can whistle while breathing in and out of an open mouth.

New Mexico - <u>Sun Pose</u> for the symbol on the state flag.

New York - In honor of the Big Apple, teacher or students may bring in apples for prosperity meditation, infusing the apples with thoughts of abundance, or serve apples for snacks. Alternately bring in roses to smell for the state flower, a rose.

North Carolina - <u>Airplane Pose</u> in honor of the first flight by the Wright Brothers. Stand on one foot, lift the other foot behind and extend arms out to the sides. This is close to a Warrior III Pose.

North Dakota - <u>Fish Pose</u> for the state fish the Northern Pike.

Ohio – <u>Archer Pose</u> for the 17 arrows on the state seal.

Oklahoma - <u>Bundle Roll</u>. Imitate the circling of a tornado and roll around on the floor with the body held together in a tight bundle.

Oregon – <u>Bug Pose</u>. With all the forest in Oregon, there's bound to be bugs. (Unrelated fun fact: The world's largest fungus grows in Oregon and is the size of 1,600 football fields.)

Pennsylvania - Liberty Bell. Stand on the feet and <u>lean from side to side</u> like a bell ringing.

Rhode Island – <u>Shell Pose</u> for a state on the coast. Shell is like baby pose but with wide knees and wide arms. The official symbol for the state is quahog, or Large Clam.

South Carolina – <u>Dolphin Pose</u> for the coastal state.

South Dakota – <u>Bow Pose</u>. Stretch like your back is a bow.

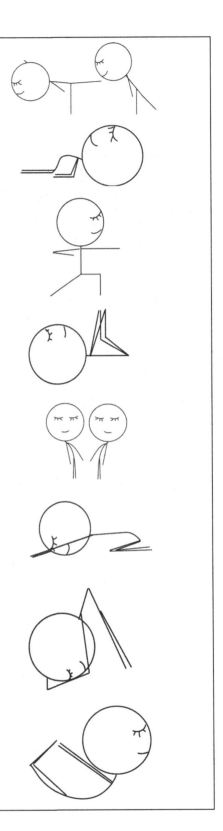

Tennessee – <u>Dance</u> and pretend you're in Nashville. Pick fun, uplifting music.

Texas – <u>Cobra Pose</u>. There's a snake in my boot!

Utah - <u>Skiing Pose</u>. Jump moving the feet from side to side in a twisting motion to mimic skiing down a hill.

Vermont – <u>Butterfly Pose</u> because it's the state insect.

Virginia - <u>Warrior Pose</u> because this is the only state to have a warrior on its flag.

West Virginia – <u>Mountain Pose</u> for the "Mountain State" where the Appalachian Mountain range is found.

Washington - Windshield Wiper pose is needed because there's lots of rain in this state. Lie down on your back feet the width of the mat, <u>move knees from side to side</u> like windshield wipers.

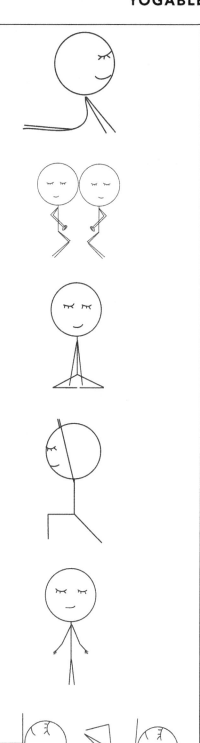

Wisconsin - <u>Cat-Cow</u> in honor of the state and its dairy farms.
People who live in Wisconsin are nicknamed "Cheeseheads."

Wyoming - <u>Lizard Pose</u>. The Horned Lizard is the state reptile.

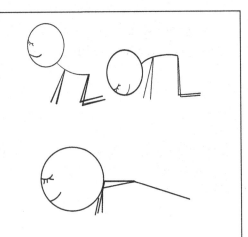

Holidays

Valentine's Day

<u>Prayer Pose at the heart center</u> – Place palms together at the center of the chest for a calm heart.

<u>Heart *Mudra*</u> – From Prayer Pose see if you can make your hands into the shape of a heart with the fingertips touching.

<u>Warrior Pose</u> – Warrior for a brave heart.

<u>Archer Pose</u> – Pretend you are Cupid's bow and arrow.

<u>Cupid Pose</u> – Stand on one leg and extend the opposite arm straight out in front, switch sides.

<u>Standing Knee Hug</u> – Stand and hug one knee into the chest while balancing, switch sides.

<u>Bow Pose</u> – The bow to the arrow.

<u>Kiss the Clouds</u> – Sit in Easy Pose, lift the chin and blow kisses up into the clouds. This is great for the neck muscles and skin!

<u>Dance</u> – Glow sticks are optional.

<u>Bountiful, Beautiful, Blissful Meditation</u> – Fold the hands at the heart and sing from the heart center.

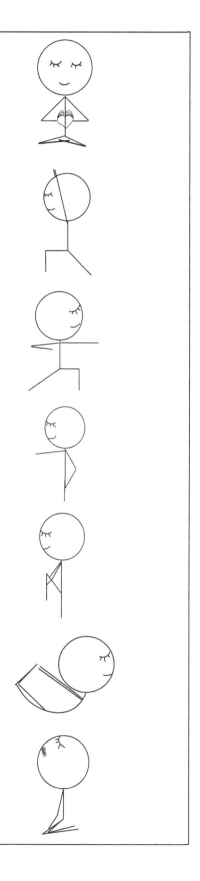

Halloween

One of my favorites! Invite students to dress up in costume if it's appropriate for the space.

Cross Crawls – pick a few of your favorite and warm up!

Spooky Night Whistle Breath – create the mood for spooky fun with a Whistle Breath.

Creaky Gate Spinal Twist with Arms Extended – Twist from side to side with arms extended, and make squeaking noises like a creaking gate.

Tree Pose or Modified Tree Pose – Stand on feet, lift the arms in the air and sway in the wind from side to side and from front to back. To make it challenging try doing this on tip toes!

Spider Pose – A Crow Squat with the hands out in front of the feet and fingers spread wide.

Zombie Neck Rolls – Roll your head in a circle like a zombie, switch directions.

Witch's Broom Spinal Twist- Bring the arms overhead with the palms together and twist from side to side. You're in the shape of a witch's broom.

Witches Brew Pelvic Rotation – Circle the torso on the pelvis like you're stirring a cauldron! Be sure to ask students what they are brewing in their cauldrons.

Cat Pose – Meow! Add the cow for a stretch in both directions.

Bat Pose – Sit in Butterfly Pose and then lie back on the ground with the arms extended straight out to each side.

Mummy Pose with Leg Lifts – Lie on the ground on your back and cross your arms over your chest like a mummy and begin to do leg lifts, either alternate legs or both at the same time.

Sensory Activity – Pumpkins work well for a sensory experience. Explore the outside and inside of the pumpkin with sight, smell and touch.

Dance – Put on some fun Halloween themed music and dance. (Glow sticks are a huge hit in this class, but are optional.)

St. Patrick's Day

Google St. Patrick's Day yoga and you'll soon find out there's nothing suitable to teach in an actual yoga class, let alone to children. However, there is a fun way to engage the students during this week. There's an old tale about leprechauns sneaking into dwellings, creating a mess, and leaving treasure behind. I like to arrive at the studio early and mess up the yoga room by throwing around the mats, blankets and blocks, and then I hide green pencils, gold coins (real, plastic, or candy), shamrock necklaces, etc. in the mess. When the kids come in, they have to clean up the mess made by the leprechauns in order to set up for class, and they get to keep any treasures they find. I recommend yoga postures that include backbends, heart openers, balancing, Rag Doll swings as found in Chapter 5, and blowing kisses up at an imaginary rainbow.

Easter

A fun Easter theme class activity is to create an Easter egg hunt. Plastic eggs can be filled with small animal figurines, or animal photos printed on paper, and then hidden around the area where yoga will be practiced. The students hunt for the eggs and take turns opening their egg to discover the posture inside. I instruct students how many eggs they are to find so that each person has the same number of eggs. I typically fill the eggs with a treat they can keep.

Fall Harvest/Thanksgiving - Take postures from **Farm Yoga** and add gratitude.

Smelling or Sensory Activity – Decorative gourds are a fun tactile prop in the fall because of their bumpy, unusual texture, and cinnamon is a yummy smell for fall.

Affirmation of Thanks – Go around the room and invite students to share what they are thankful for in their lives. You'd be surprised, but even non-verbal kids can participate in this because they can be assisted by their parent or yoga partner. They get it, and know what brings them happiness in their lives.

Winter Solstice/Christmas

Put together a fun winter holiday class! Use suggested postures from the **Winter Yoga** theme class, and add singing and dancing for a celebration.

A Christmas theme class that my students enjoy is reading a Christmas themed children's book and doing yoga postures to match the story. What they like even better is when I modify the story by adding their names to it with the specific postures that they personally enjoy!

More class ideas:
1. Read a children's book that has plenty of animals and movement and coordinate yoga postures to the story.

2. Play songs that are familiar to the targeted age group and coordinate yoga postures to go along with the words of the song.
3. A multitude of children's yoga storybooks and yoga cards can be found online.

Options for babies and toddlers:

All movements are to be gentle, never forced, honoring the developmental stage of the little ones. The following is a short list of yogic ideas for babies and/or toddlers that can be practiced without any pressure of time or perfection.

1. Practice animal postures that toddlers are able to imitate.
2. Sit child in the lap and lean them side to side while singing.
3. With the child on the floor, or sitting in the lap, move the arms across the body in a criss-cross motion. In the same position you can also move opposite arms up and down. Move the legs this way too.
4. Gently massage the hands and arms.
5. Gently squeeze the fingertips to replicate the action of Kirtan Kriya.
6. Sing often. Sing songs, or sing a narrative about what you are doing. For example, sing about making a salad when preparing dinner.

Fun and Functional Additions:

Earlier in the book, I put the kibosh on traditional yoga props (I've literally witnessed a yoga strap turn into a sling shot to the face). I do, however, totally encourage the use of what I will call non-traditional props in order to enhance a full-body experience. If you've scanned through the themed classes, you get the idea of using all five senses for experience. Adding non-traditional props to yoga classes can engage young people in their yoga practice.

These additions are completely optional, and many can be found in your own home, making them cost effective. I suggest using the fun and functional items sparsely, however, as you don't want to overwhelm your students by lumping them all together in a single class. Think of incorporating all 5 senses, but not all at one time.

Sight: The classes are visual, special props can be seen, and we use ASL for the Long Time Sun Song. Glow sticks are a favorite visual effect! If you can reconcile the waste created by discarded glow sticks and their impact on the environment with the pure joy they bring to class, they may be purchased in craft or toy stores, or even at some local drug or grocery stores. Turn down the lights and dance or meditate in their subtle, soothing glow. Relate the glow of the stick to the students own inner light. If the sticks break, don't worry, the glowing liquid does not leave lasting stains and poison control says ingestion is non-toxic. I'm not sure these are facts I even want to know, but the yoga studio has, in fact, looked like a glowing crime scene in the dark. And, yes, I know a young boy who consumed the liquid inner contents of a glow stick. Thankfully, the ingestion was not under my watch.

Hearing: Following class instruction, mantra, music, and the gong stimulate listening. Adding a sea shell, rain-stick, or the snapping of fingers provides for an added hearing experience as well as touch.

Students can make their own "rain sticks" in class by filling an empty cardboard paper towel tube with a stick or rolled up foil and adding ½ cup of dry beans and/or rice, then covering the open end with a strip of duct tape. Make sure to cover one end first before pouring the bean and/or rice mixture inside. Finally, decorate the outside of the tube as desired. I provide stickers and crayons for decoration to avoid a big, colorful or sticky mess in the yoga space.

Touch: As students participate in class, they have a variety of tactile experiences. Using different textured animals, sponges, pine cones, seashells, fruit, vegetables, etc., makes class interesting. When offering a tactile experience, I ask questions and model descriptive language, *"How does this feel? Is it bumpy, soft, hard, etc.?"* Crystals and stones may be used during class for the sensory experience as well as their healing and grounding properties.

Smell: Items in themed classes can be smelled, such as flowers and fruits. Aromatherapy with pure essential oils may be used in class, too. This serves two purposes: first, the targeted effect the aroma has depending on the oils being used, and second, the aromas help to stimulate deeper breathing. Always get permission before using any scents in class.

Taste: Breathing in through the mouth, such as in Lion Breath stimulates taste and sensation in the mouth. Additionally, seasonal treats, fruits, or drinks may be brought into class to be shared with parent permission.

Aromatherapy

Essential oils can be diffused throughout class or used at designated times with specific intent. They can be used at the beginning of class, in the middle during a class theme, or at the end of class for deep relaxation. Oils can be breathed, spritzed, or applied topically by massage. I personally do not touch students, but let the parents apply massage pressure to kids and to themselves. Make sure to use a pure quality essential oil with no fillers.

To breathe in, mix the oils in a small container with some Himalayan rock salt. The container may be passed around and the students can breathe in the smell. Porous lava rock works too.

To spritz, dilute the oils in purified water and fill a small spray bottle with the mixture. Spritz the spray mix over and around students as they settle in for deep relaxation. Avoid spraying too close to the face.

To apply topically, add the essential oils to a carrier oil such as grapeseed or almond oil, then fill a small pump or flip-top bottle with the mixture. Dispense a bit of the oil blend to each parent or caregiver to massage into the ankles, tops of the feet, and lower legs of their children (adult kids too), then dispense a little more for the parent or caregiver. Avoid using essential oils on areas of the body that may be rubbed into the eyes or ingested, like the hands, arms, or face.

Always ask permission before using any essential oil in yoga. If anyone in the class is opposed/allergic to using essential oils, then simply leave this option out.

Recommended Essential Oils
Orange Oil - helps to reduce anxiety
Peppermint Oil - boosts awareness, elevates mood
Orange/Peppermint Blend - increases focus
Wintergreen - good for the sensory system, increases sensory awareness (do not use topically or ingest)
Rosemary - helps with concentration and creativity
Rosemary/Lemon Blend - makes a nice spritz for creative flow
Patchouli - supports communication
Lavender - calming and relaxing
Cedarwood - helps with sleep
Lavender/Cedarwood Blend - makes a cozy spritz to use for deep relaxation
Sandalwood - encourages relaxation and mental clarity

A Few Good Stones

Hematite – This magnetic stone may also be known as "rattlesnake eggs" due to its sizzling magnetic nature. Hematite stones or "rattlesnake eggs" may be used for grounding during deep relaxation by placing a stone in each hand. Hematite helps to absorb negative energy as well as to calm stress and worry. I recommend Autistic individuals carry this stone on the person.

Sugilite – This stone of love may help with the issues of anger, temper, struggles with fear and difficulty in connecting with others. It may help to support and regulate balance in the nervous system. For those with Autism, I recommend carrying this stone on the person or placing in the bedroom.

Selenite - A self-clearing crystal that supports protection and good luck. It has a healing effect, removes negativity, and strengthens the aura, and can be used in class either by touch, or by waving a Selenite wand over the students during deep relaxation or at the end of class.

Rose Quartz – A good rock to have in the yoga space, it promotes the energy of compassion, healing, peace and love. It also helps in releasing fears.

Amethyst – This beautiful purple rock helps with anxiety, depression, and overthinking. Polished Amethyst can make a great "worry stone" as it is smooth and can be rubbed between the fingers or held in the palm with the intention to release irritation and increase calm.

Any of the aforementioned crystals can be held and admired with direct contact or be placed in the home as decoration. If the stones are distracting or at risk of being put in the mouth please use caution when using with children. Small stones can be sewn into seams or hidden pockets in clothing or backpacks. If you have a child who finds everything, I advise avoiding the hiding tactic and simply take crystals or stones out with supervision. I have one sweet, teenage Autistic student who can find even the tiniest stone hidden under his mattress. He doesn't miss a thing!

My son received a small Sugilite stone as a gift, and likes to carry it with him in a pocket. He has rules for this gift, only carrying it in a pocket that has a snap so it won't fall out, and putting it on his nightstand at bedtime. Recently he took the stone out of his pocket and put it on the dining room table. That night we had a dish with black beans, and at the end of the meal he picked up a stray bean to pop in his mouth. Turns out the bean was actually his Sugilite stone! Ingestion was avoided and we all had a good laugh. He is an adult and thought it was hysterical, but this short story is a reminder to be mindful with gem stones and kids.

Be mindful in all areas and honor your students. Show up with your authentic self, come from your heart, and be open to an amazing experience. I sincerely hope you enjoy the family yoga classes I have shared in this chapter. Keep it simple, and remember - have fun!

As you may have noticed by now, the central idea for presenting yoga to any population with special considerations begins with the word "yes." Say yes - show up and deliver. Don't be afraid to make mistakes. We can carry the load collectively.

A closing guided meditation, *I am Perfect Exactly as I am* by Louise Hay: (2000)

"I am perfect exactly as I am. I am neither too much or too little. I do not have to prove to anyone or anything who I am. I have been many identities, each one a perfect expression for that particular lifetime. I am content to be who and what I am this time. I do not yearn to be like someone else, for that is not the expression I chose this time. Next time I will be different. I am perfect as I am, right now. I am sufficient. I am one with all of life. There is no need to struggle to be better. All I need to do is love myself more today than yesterday, and to treat myself as someone who is deeply loved. With joy, I recognize my perfection and the perfection of life."

Closing Reflections

Chapter 9, this chapter, originally ended with the above guided meditation by Louise Hay, *I am Perfect Exactly as I am*. As I sit down to write now, it was a week ago that my editor informed me the ending was too abrupt. I agreed, but also balked, maintaining that my ending message is that we are all perfect as we are right now. My editor suggested I write an ending expressing my gratitude for the wonderful experience teaching over many years. Only yesterday I responded to her, saying I would add an appropriate closing, but not wanting to simply paraphrase the introduction, I would wait for inspiration. Well, less than 24 hours later the inspiration has been revealed.

My closing reflections literally came from a reflection of light. Last night we received much needed rain here in Southern California. It poured all night, the electricity is out this morning, I'm writing in a spiral bound notebook with a cheap ballpoint pen, and I am inspired.

After the full night of rain, the morning was crisp and bright, with blue sky, puffy, white clouds, and a dusting of snow on the mountains behind my home. I wandered out into the backyard to admire the raindrops collected on the plants. Rain always adds a little sparkle to the garden. In one corner of the garden, I came across a small succulent that stood out among the others. In the middle of this succulent a small pool of raindrops had coalesced into a single, shining gem. It actually looked like a large diamond. This single, clear, liquid jewel reflected the sun, showing off its multifaceted surface and revealing its mirror like depth. This was my inspiration, and a metaphor for life.

Humanity is multifaceted, just like a fine gem or a shiny raindrop. Each individual has their own expression or vibration that is perfect for them, which helps them to deliver their unique gifts to the world. As individuals we pool and coalesce into the whole of humanity. Each of our personal projections come together divinely for this time and space. Together we make one. Yoga is like this too. At its essence it is union, a blending of body, mind, and spirit, and a technology that paves the way for us to shine from the inside out.

So yes, I am deeply grateful to teach yoga to people of all levels and abilities. Even better than the gratitude is that I am often left in awe and wonder by these beautiful souls. My ultimate invitation is to release preconceived ideas of limitation, embrace the now, and enjoy this great big pulse of life.

Music

A helpful companion soundtrack titled *Yogable* is available to guide you through the yoga practice. Proper pronunciation of the mantras is given, and the music provides a follow along for the practice. If music is unavailable, the meditations may be done with the focus on the breath, in most cases a long, deep breath.

The soundtrack *Yogable* has been recorded by yoga teacher, teacher trainer, and recording artist Jap Dharam Rose. All songs were produced and recorded by Thomas Barquee at Zen Den Studio in Los Angeles, California. The soundtrack may be purchased at cdbaby.com and found on other streaming platforms.

References

Chapter One
Gurucharan Singh Khalsa, Ph.D., from live teachings, Los Angeles 2018

Chapter Two
Jowett, Geoffrey, The Power of I AM, Aligning the Chakras of Consciousness. Divine Arts 2014
Bruyere, Rosalyn L., *Wheels of Light, Chakras, Auras, and the Healing Energy of the Body*. Fireside, Simon & Shuster, Inc. 1994
Bhajan, Yogi, *The Aquarian Teacher*: *Kundalini Research Institute International Kundalini Yoga Teacher Training Level I,* Kundalini Research Institute 2003
Abraham-Hicks, Esther, *The Autistic Revolution: Children of the Time of Awakening* [DVD], Abraham-Hicks Publications, Law of Attraction Workshops 2008

Chapter Three
Rumi, The Essential Rumi, New Expanded Edition, trans. Coleman Barks. Harper Collins 2003.
Bhajan, Yogi, *The Aquarian Teacher: Kundalini Research Institute International Kundalini Yoga Teacher Training Level l,* Kundalini Research Institute 2003

Chapter Four
Thich Nhat Hanh, In Thich Nhat Hanh Quote Collective 2019
Mejia, Michael, *Breathe*, The Poetry of Michael, unpub. ms.

Chapter Five
Mejia, Michael, The Poetry of Michael, unpub.ms.

Chapter Six
Gurucharan Singh Khalsa, Ph.D., from live teachings, Los Angeles 2018
Khalsa, Santokh Singh, D.C., *Understanding Kundalini Yoga A Beginners Guide to Transforming Your Life, Kriya for Elevation,* Santokh Singh Khalsa, D.C. 2016
Khalsa, Shakta Kaur*, Kundalini Yoga Unlock Your Inner Potential Through Life-Changing Exercise, Kriya for Pelvic Balance & Kriya for Strengthening the Aura.* Dorling Kindersley 2001 (childrensyoga.com)
Kirtan Kriya Meditation in Alzheimer's Research & Prevention Foundation Handbook 2018
Khalsa, Gururattan Kaur, Ph.D. and Ann Marie Maxwell, *Relax and Renew, Anti-Hypertension Meditation.* copyright December 1988 www.yogatech.com/Guru Rattana PhD/Relax_and_ Renew
Khalsa, GuruMeher, *Senses of The Soul Emotional Therapy for Strength, Healing and Guidance, Safeguard Your Heart Exercise.* Kundalini Research Institute 2013

Chapter Seven

Chodron, Pema, Shambhala Sun Magazine 2009

Guru for the Aquarian Age, The Life and Teachings of Guru Nanak. Yogiji Press, Brotherhood of Life Books 1996

Khalsa, Dharma Sing, M.D., and Stauth, Cameron, *Meditation as Medicine, Activate the Power of Your Natural Healing Force.* Fireside 2001

Khalsa Gururattan Kaur, Ph.D., and Maxwell, Ann Marie, *Relax and Renew, Warm Up Exercise Set & Exercises for Maintaining a Flexible Spine* copyright December 1988. www.yogatech.com/Guru_Rattana PhD/Relax_and_Renew

Khalsa, GuruMeher, *Senses of The Soul Emotional Therapy for Strength, Healing and Guidance, The Mind, At Wits End Exercise.* Kundalini Research Institute 2013

Khalsa, Shakta Kaur, *Kundalini Yoga Unlock Your Inner Potential Through Life-Changing Exercise, Meditation for a Calm Heart.* Dorling Kindersley 2001 (childrensyoga.com)

Chapter Eight

Mejia, Michael, The Poetry of Michael, unpub. ms.

Bernstein, Gabrielle, *The Universe Has Your Back, Transform Fear to Faith.* Hay House Inc. 2016

Grandin, Temple, cf. www.autismspeaks.org

Benton, Mehtab, *Gong Yoga, Healing and Enlightenment Through Sound.* iUniverse Inc. 2008

Khalsa, Hari Kirn Kaur, "Celestial Communication" from live teachings, Los Angeles 2020 & 2021

Rose, Jap Dharam, Recording Artist, www.japdharamrose.com soundtracks from 2016, 2019, 2021

Chapter Nine

Rogers, Fred, from speech delivered at Dartmouth College Commencement June 2002, as transcribed by www.dartmouth.edu

Khalsa, Shakta Kaur, *Balloon Breath* as referenced on childrensyoga.com

Hay, Louise, Guided Meditation in *Inner Wisdom, Meditations for the Heart and Soul, I am Perfect Exactly as I Am.* Hay House Inc. 2000

Resources

Alzheimer's Research and Prevention Foundation
www.alzheimersprevention.org

Resources for more yoga and meditation:

3HO – Healthy Happy Holy Organization
www.3ho.org

Khalsa, Gururattan Kaur, Ph.D., *Relax and Renew*
www.yogatech.com

Khalsa, Shakta Kaur, *Kundalini Yoga*
www.childrensyoga.com

KRI – Kundalini Research Institute
www.kundaliniresearchinstitute.org

Library of Teachings
www.libraryofteachings.com

Printed in the United States
by Baker & Taylor Publisher Services